Liszt

Cover design and art direction by Pearce Marchbank Studio.
Cover photography by Julian Hawkins.

Printed and bound in Hungary

© Bryce Morrison 1989.
This edition published in 1989 by Omnibus Press, a division of Book Sales Limited.

Hardback
Order No. OP44072
ISBN 0.7119.1033.2

Softback
Order No. OP44999
ISBN 0.7119.1682.9

Exclusive Distributors:
Book Sales Limited,
8/9 Frith Street,
London W1V 5TZ,
England.
Music Sales Pty Limited,
120 Rothschild Avenue,
Rosebery,
Sydney,
NSW 2018,
Australia.
To The Music Trade Only:
Music Sales Limited,
8/9 Frith Street,
London W1V 5TZ,
England.
Music Sales Corporation,
24 East 22nd Street,
New York,
NY10010,
U.S.A.

The Illustrated Lives of the Great Composers.

Liszt

Bryce Morrison

Omnibus Press
London/New York/Sydney/Cologne

For Burrett and Henrietta McBee
and in memory of those incomparable
New Hampshire Christmases.

Contents

Selected Bibliography

Armando, Walter G. Franz Liszt. Hamburg, 1961.

Bache, Constance (editor). Liszt's Letters. London, 1894.

Beckett, Walter. Liszt. London, 1956.

Bory, Robert. *Une retraite romantique en Suisse*. Geneva, 1923.

Bory, Robert. *La vie de Franz Liszt*. Paris, 1936.

Fay, Amy. Music Study in Germany. New York, 1965.

Hallé, Sir Charles. Life and Letters. London, 1896.

Hervey, Arthur. Franz Liszt. London, 1911.

Hill, Ralph. Liszt. London, 1936.

Huneker, James. Liszt. London, 1911.

La Mara (pseudonym, Marie Lipsius). *Liszt's Briefe*, 8 vols. Leipzig, 1893-4.

Liszt, Franz. The Letters of Franz Liszt to Marie zu Sayn-Wittgenstein. Translated and edited by Howard E Hugo. Harvard, 1963.

Liszt, Franz. The Gipsy in Music. Translated by Edwin Evans. 2 vols. London, 1926.

Liszt, Franz. Life of Chopin. Translated by M.W. Cook. London 1877.

Liszt, Franz. Life of Chopin. Translated by John Broadhouse. London, 1912.

Mackenzie, Sir Alexander. A Musician's Narrative. London, 1918.

Newman, Ernest. The Man Liszt. London, 1934.

Olliver, Blandine. *Liszt, le musician passionné*. Paris, 1936.

Perenni, E. Liszt. London, 1975.

Philip, I. *La Technique de Franz Liszt*. 5 vols. Paris, 1932.

Raabe, Peter. *Franz Liszt: Leben und Schaffen*. 2 vols. Stuttgart, 1968.

Rellstab, Ludwig. F. Liszt. Berlin, 1842.

Searle, Humphrey. The Music of Liszt. New York, 1966.

Sitwell, Sacheverell. Liszt. London, 1955.

Storr, Anthony, The Dynamics of Creation. London, 1972.

Strelezki, Anton. Personal recollections of chats with Liszt. London, 1983.

Szabolcsi, Bence. The Twilight of Liszt. Budapest, 1956.

Taylor, Ronald. Franz Liszt: The Man and the Musician. London, 1986.

Walker, Alan. Franz Liszt: The Man and his Music. London, 1970.

Walker, Alan. Franz Liszt: Vol. 1 The Virtuoso Years, 1811-1847. London, 1983.

Acknowledgements

It would be impossible for me to mention all those who helped to shape and colour this book. Indirect help and influence came from many sources, and the rigours of research, in the British and Bodleian Libraries, were invariably complemented by informal talk – often into the small hours – with friends and colleagues. I quickly came to value the comments of those who love "to fold their legs and have out their talk" as much as a more impersonal, strenuous and severe procedure.

In this sense I am grateful to Paul Crossley, whose annotations to both his recitals and recordings said more than many books. His recent television talk, 'the heart in pilgrimage', in which he traced Liszt's arduous attempt to reach 'a state of grace', made many Lisztians think again and positively forbade all complacency. Alfred Brendel's insistence that Liszt is among the great composers was made with rare wit and originality and, *per contra*, Vladimir Ashkenazy's no less impassioned belief that Liszt is an inferior composer whose music is alive with surplus bravura provided a valuable stimulus of disagreement; a true case of point counter point.

More formally, I have to thank Alastair, Marquess of Londonderry who, in inviting me to lecture at his memorable Liszt Festival at Wynyard Park, prompted some useful revisions and reflections; Jorge Bolet, for so generously taking time off from an impossible schedule to provide the Preface; Robert Matthew-Walker for first reading the text with such care and interest; and Didier de Cottignies, who provided me with Mrs. B Crosti's previously unpublished photograph of Liszt for the frontispiece.

19, Hinde House
11, Hinde Street,
London, W.1.   Bryce Morrison, 1986

A creative person is one who possesses an unusual combination of qualities rather than one particular attribute. It is the tension between these opposites, and the need to resolve this tension which provides the positive force for creation. (Anthony Storr).

All great writing springs from *le dur désir de durer*, the harsh contrivance of spirit against death, the hope to overreach time by force of creation. "Brightness falls from the air;" five words and a trick of darkening sound. But they have outworn three centuries. (George Steiner).

Foreword

This succinct study of the life and times of Franz Liszt represents an important contribution to the biographies of this great genius already in existence. It is not a detailed chronological recounting of events as so many others have been but rather an intricate review of the significant events and situations that influenced Liszt and made him the complex, multifaceted personality that he became.

Of all the great figures of Romanticism Liszt is, perhaps, the one that exerted the most direct influence on his contemporaries and the Romantic movement as a whole. He was certainly the greatest innovator of his time; performing in public without a score, playing a whole recital, as we do today, without other assisting artists; changing the traditional placement of the piano on the concert platform, and lastly, developing and inventing a new musical form, the Symphonic Poem. He was an indefatigable champion of new music, promoting and performing the works of those in whom he believed.

I congratulate Mr Morrison on his use of lengthy quotations from Liszt's writings and those of his contemporaries. It gives his work a seal of authenticity which many other biographies lack.

The reader will find this work a fascinating account of that incomparable period in the history of music 1811-1886.

Jorge Bolet.

Preface

Liszt is a biographer's dream or nightmare. Outrageously gifted from birth and clearly destined to dazzle and astound, he also exhibited from an early age a deeply divided nature that attracted a no less divided opinion or estimate. Not surprisingly, Liszt's larger-than-life brilliance rested on uncertain foundations and the fruits of such a background were uneven and controversial. Liszt's life and work are inseparable and have tended to provoke either an uncomprehending hostility, unsatisfactory hysteria or uncritical adulation.

Simple yet sophisticated, naïve yet cunning, mean-spirited yet generous to a fault, Liszt's essential complexity has always needed protection as much from his most ardent devotees as from his most savage enemies, from over-zealous and sentimental guardians of his supposed spirituality as well as those (like Ernest Newman) whose prickly nature over-reacted to such a scintillating and idealised legend. Mr Newman's infamous book is hardly a work of victimisation in the sense of, say Middleton Murry's *Son of Woman*, a study of D.H. Lawrence. He, after all, had no personal axe to grind. But, provoked by sentimentality, he endeavoured to present altogether harder, more durable if less palatable truths, seeing Liszt's undoubted streak of opportunism and vulgarity as of paramount importance.

The truth, as usual, exists somewhere between and at the risk of seeming unfashionably psychological I would like to suggest that while Liszt undoubtedly created out of a contradictory, yet comprehensible mixture of religious zeal and vainglorious mastery he also wrote out of a profound sense of inner uncertainty and disharmony. The facts of his life point inevitably to such a state which can, however, be seen in a positive rather than a negative light.

Earlier than most artists Liszt experienced a divine discontent and his creativity became his essential key to survival. Through his endlessly evolving art he found profound solace and a symbolic and

Liszt (previously unpublished photograph by B. Crosti).

acute resolution of such uneasiness. Compelled to create with a truly phenomenal speed and energy he mirrored and crystallised in his art every fleeting nuance of his life, of his teeming intellect and imagination. And if the results were inevitably uneven, less perfect than, say, Chopin's, they can also be seen to reflect a greater magnanimity, breadth, scope and generosity of spirit.

Again, although it is often true that art can be a substitute for reality, an escapist fantasy dangerously remote from day to day concerns, with Liszt the two are inseparable, a vital 'interinanimation' that fuels the constant ebb and flow, the flux and torment of his creativity. In this particular case I therefore feel disinclined to question T.S. Eliot's famous assumption that "the more perfect the artist the more completely separate in him will be the man who suffers and the man who creates." It is surely Liszt's chief glory that he was never a "perfect" artist.

That Liszt's colossally energetic work and lifestyle should cost him incalculable pain is an added and ironic corollary. And although it is true of a great many artists that what we chiefly admire so many years later was often the culmination of intense early and personal suffering, Liszt, as much as any composer, represents a unique and peculiarly absorbing case. His sudden sicknesses and withdrawals form their own tacit but eloquent testimony to his disturbed and shifting state of mind. His lifelong vacillation between worldly acclaim and spiritual seclusion, the constant friction between the personal and public sides of his nature, are invariably at the centre of his many crises. And one of the odder and most profound products of such inner torment were those still controversial dark-hued experiments of his final years, music of a strange, haunted and austere prophecy. The vexed question of this ever surprising journey from what has been called *l'exubérance de coeur* to *l'amertume de coeur* was initially answered with gleeful contempt by Liszt's many enemies; irrefutable evidence of shallowness leading to senility. But *Nuages Gris, Unstern* or *La Lugubre Gondola* 1 and 2 (their very titles significant of Liszt's inner desolation and loneliness during his final years) represent an assured journey into the unknown, courageous acts of faith and the creation of what Liszt was fond of calling his musical afterlife. By his own confession Liszt's final ambition was to hurl a lance as far as possible into the boundless realm of the future.

Less personally, such music also reflects Liszt's self-conscious attempt to break with convention. Having already scandalised such die-hard conservatives as Brahms and Mendelssohn he turned his back for ever on tradition and with a knowledge and foresight that in retrospect are truly astonishing, freed himself from the restraints of balance, symmetry and form, experimenting freely instead with such novelties and unmentionables as atonality, asymmetry, dissonance and a startling and seemingly perverse sense of incompleteness. The sequence and repetition that form an essential part, for example, of works such as the Third Mephisto Waltz, the Mephisto Polka or the *Bagatelle sans tonalitée* only further and ironically emphasise the music's diablerie and cunning oddity of expression. Confronted by such seeming whimsicality Liszt's contemporaries saw him as a dangerous apostle of chaos advocating self-indulgence rather than true art. It was left to a later generation of composers, notably Debussy, Bartók and Stravinsky, to access and admire more accurately Liszt's courage and prophetic strength, his profound inner indifference to adversity whatever the cost. Liszt's peculiar and distinctive compositional methods seemed in no way disturbing or disconcerting to those for whom the Debussyan or Stravinskyian revolutions were simply musical facts of life.

It has also been left to our age to appreciate more fully Liszt's multifaceted nature, a man whose strength grew from weakness and whose greatness flourished out of confusion. Certainly if we think of Liszt as a Don Juan forced into awareness of the spiritual side of life, or a virtuous man haunted by the 'shadow' side of his personality, we come closer to understanding the distinctive quality and complexity of his genius.

Liszt's mother, Anna.

Liszt's birthplace at Raiding.

Liszt in 1820 wearing the Hungarian national costume given him by Prince Esterházy.

Chapter 1

The Early Years: prodigy and *wunderkind*

Liszt was arguably the greatest of all virtuosi and his *glanz*, or glitter years (1839-47), have been described as "unmatched in the history of performance." His childhood and early years are therefore of particular importance and interest. Here lay the seeds of future greatness, and although Liszt was hardly the sort of *Wunderkind* of whom the child remains and the wonder vanishes (Godowsky's sarcastic reduction of prodigies), it is already possible to observe a disturbing thread running through a superficially conventional narrative. The pattern of Liszt's life was formed early and suggested many of the more unsettling aspects of the classic child prodigy's state. Even Liszt's early and phenomenal success was clouded by more than just transient psychological pain and confusion.

Liszt's grandfather.

Liszt's ancestry remains vague, and although he fondly imagined himself to be of the Hungarian nobility he was more likely of basic peasant stock. His grandfather, George Adam Liszt (born in Edelsthal, a small village near Pressburg) married three times and had twenty-five children and his father, also called Adam (1776-1827), worked as a steward at Raiding on the Esterházy estate, described as "a cultural Paradise" standing in complete isolation in view of the great Hungarian plains, fifty miles from Vienna. More significantly, Adam Liszt had been a Franciscan novice at the age of nineteen before being dismissed from the order for "inconsistent and variable character," and his intense love of music (particularly of Haydn, and of Hummel's piano playing) was frustrated by his mundane position and occupation.

Liszt's mother, Anna Lager (1788-1866) a south German who Adam Liszt married at the age of thirty, though undoubtedly a model wife and mother, remains a more shadowy figure; a mere adjunct to her husband and the brilliant life he quickly envisaged for his son ("My son, you are predestined! You will realise that artistic goal

Liszt in 1825.

Prince Nicolas
Esterházy.

Carl Czerny.

Haydn.

Liszt's father.

whose spell bewitched my youth in vain.")

Liszt himself was born at Raiding on October 22, 1811, the year of the Comet and a suitable portent for a unique and trail-blazing career. By the time he was six, much to his father's joy, Liszt showed an obsessive love for music and particularly for the piano. He could read music long before he knew the alphabet. What was drudgery for other children acquired an intense magic for him and a portrait of Beethoven at once took on a glowing and peculiar significance. Nervous and highly-wrought from the start, the colour and

17

excitement of Liszt's early life was countered by sudden illnesses that came and went in inexplicable fashion.

At the age of nine Liszt played a Concerto by Ferdinand Ries and a free Fantasia of his own composition with such success that a subscription was set up to help with future studies and it quickly became necessary to look towards wider horizons than those of provincial Raiding. Vienna in particular seemed a cultural Mecca and, according to Sir W.H. Hadow, represented one of the three greatest periods of history (the others being Periclean Athens and Elizabethan England). Suitable tutors were approached including Hummel who priced himself out of the market and out of musical history as Liszt's teacher. The indefatigable Carl Czerny, who taught from 8am to 8pm and who composed over a thousand opuses, was more generous as well as more perceptive and after initially refusing Liszt as a student he heard him play and rapidly changed his mind. Czerny initially found Liszt's playing

quite irregular, untidy, confused, and he had so little idea of fingering that he threw his fingers quite arbitrarily all over the keyboard. But that notwithstanding, I was astonished by the talent which Nature had bestowed on him

Vienna.

Liszt's gifts may have been wild and untutored at this early stage but they were clearly already extraordinary and Czerny took his young and undisciplined charge firmly in hand. For the first time Liszt was criticised rather than praised and his coltish facility was properly focused only after strong resistance. The composer of *The School of Velocity* would not tolerate a vague approximation to the text and, in time, Liszt learnt to be grateful for the backbreaking régime of technique, of basic scales and arpeggios. Later, provoked by a variety of inspirations and notably by Paganini's diablerie, he supplemented and far exceeded Czerny's limited skills and laid the foundations of one of the most superhuman techniques of all time.

Liszt's progress was exceptionally rapid and soon Czerny was able to say, "never before had I had so eager, talented, or industrious a student. After only a year I could let him perform publicly, and he aroused a degree of enthusiasm in Vienna that few artists have equalled." Certainly by 1822 Liszt's piano playing no longer sounded like brilliant sight-reading and his two concerts prompted not only references to "a little Hercules who has, as it were, fallen from the clouds" but also fulfilled even his teacher's ultra-precise standards and ideals. His gifts were compared to the infant Mozart's and Beethoven's and it is from this time that the story of Beethoven's kiss emanates. This "artistic christening", referring to a private rather than public occasion, occurred after Liszt had played Beethoven the first movement of his C major Piano Concerto. Apparently the composer was so moved that he kissed Liszt on the forehead saying,

"Go! You are one of the fortunate ones, for you will give joy and happiness to many other people. There is nothing better or finer."

Success in Vienna proved more than congenial to both father and son but there were new cities to conquer, notably Paris. Adam Liszt's deepest wish was that his son should study at the Paris Conservatoire, and so, after further triumphs *en route* it came as a bitter blow to find his hopes prematurely dashed. No foreigners were admitted to the Conservatoire and Cherubini (the school's Principal) was unwilling to waive the rules even for Liszt. However, it took more than such inflexible bureaucracy to damage Liszt's resilience and after suitable letters from the Hungarian nobility were presented a recital was given before the city's social élite. Liszt at once became *le petit Liszt* and the

Beethoven.

Title page of Liszt's
Etudes, opus 1.   20

The 'severe' Cherubini.

darling of Paris, and his recital caused such a commotion that its effect penetrated the firmly closed doors of the Conservatoire and vibrated across the English Channel to London where there was already talk of "a musical phenomenon." Liszt had played his recital from memory, an unheard-of feat later denounced by his enemies as characteristic presumption and superficiality. Already Liszt tasted the bitter as well as the sweet fruits of success. And it was hardly surprising that "the eighth wonder of the world" who at the age of thirteen had already composed his opera, *Don Sanche*, should invite hostility as well as admiration. The pattern of things to come was formed and it was at this time that Liszt received his first poison-pen letter.

However, a trip to London was clearly necessary to confirm his status as "the greatest performer of the present day" and although his concerts were usually shared by a strange assortment of artists (including the ubiquitous Miss Symonds whose vocal specialities and lollipops included, *yes, this is the Indian drum* and *when thy bosom* he achieved his by now customary success and was rewarded with the astronomical fee of £100, an unprecedented figure in 1824. Even the British distaste for such precosity and early accomplishment was overcome and the visit included a royal concert before George IV at Windsor.

But the effects of Liszt's strange and in many ways abnormal existence began to show. His colossal but relatively easy success suddenly seemed shallow. Already, at the age of fifteen, Liszt became sombre and introspective and his diary included lengthy precepts and quotations from Saint Paul and Saint Augustine. Thus, "wasting

The more amiable
Cherubini.

Windsor Castle.

London.

time is one of the worst faults in the world. Life is so short, every moment is so precious; yet we live as if life will never end" or "there are few things which are impossible in themselves. We lack merely the application, not the means to make them succeed."

Much to his father's consternation he retreated from the public's relentless gaze and was seized with an intense longing for a religious, serene and contemplative life, startling confirmation of his belief as a child that "there was nothing so self-evident as heaven, nothing so true as the compassion of God." Subsequent acclaim in Paris (including the successful production of his opera *Don Sanche* in 1825) could not shake his resolve and Liszt was to be a haunted man for the rest of his long and turbulent life, regretting the bliss of solitude one minute and the madding crowd the next.

Don Sanche, which was lost and not rediscovered until 1903, is – not surprisingly – written in the style of Pauer, Liszt's composition teacher at the time. This, combined with the *Allegro di Bravura* and the G minor Scherzo (discovered by Busoni in 1909) and several other works, formed Liszt's earliest and most precocious composition. The Scherzo, composed within a few hours, already contains the germ of an idea that later found its truest outlet in the Nineteenth Hungarian Rhapsody (1885). More importantly, the *Douze Études*, opus 1, form a rudimentary foundation or prototype for the later and formidable *Études d'exécution transcendante*, though their Czernyesque sparkle and vitality gives little inkling of Liszt's later revolutionary brilliance and audacity. I should point out that the seeds of Liszt's truest genius took a remarkably long time to germinate. The twelve *Études* are a case in point since the opus 1 set were grandiloquently elaborated in 1838 before being greatly clarified and refined for their final version in 1851. Far more than their mere influence can be felt in Liapunov's twelve *Études d'exécution transcendante* opus 11 (1897-1905) dedicated to the memory of Franz Liszt. Indeed, Liapunov complained that Liszt's influence was so strong that it destroyed his own individuality. Liapunov's own fascinating, recognisably slavic if altogether too derivative tribute culminated in the *Elégie en memoire de Franz Liszt.*

But returning to Liszt's work, the style of all three versions has been helpfully compared by Humphrey Searle and the first and final versions most illuminatingly recorded side by side by Thomas Rajna. [CRD 1058-9]. It has also been suggested that the storm and stress of the more obviously bravura studies such as No 2 in A minor, 4 (*Mazeppa*), 6 (*Vision*), 7 (*Eroica*), 8 (*Wilde Jagd*), 10 (in F minor), and 12 (*Chasse Neige*) are countered by the lyricism and visionary simplicity of 3 (*Paysage*), the delicate tracery of 9 (*La Ricordanza*), or the harmonic fullness and daring of 11 (*Harmonies du Soir*). Even the notoriously demanding No 5 (*Feux Follets*) shows an essentially lyrical virtuosity. Thus "transcendante" implies virtuosity of poetic response as much as virtuosity of technique. It may also imply a radical advance on Czerny's classic pedagogical études or studies. Liszt's dedication of his twelve *Études d'exécution transcendante* to Czerny is both a witty and affectionate tribute to his teacher's virtues and limitations as a composer.

However assured Liszt's brilliance, the dichotomy between outward acclaim and inner desolation continued to plague him and although a third visit to London in 1827 was highly successful (his audience included Moscheles, a mediocre if greatly celebrated pianist and composer of his time) his sense of his priestly vocation grew stronger than ever. Natural gaiety gave way to a cloistral sobriety, gregariousness and love of applause to isolation, and his health, to say nothing of the family income, was increasingly jeopardised. Adam Liszt was compelled to take firm action and to his son's plea "to be granted to him the life of the saints and perhaps die the death of the martyrs" he offered a cool and sagacious reply:

because one loves a thing that is no evidence one is called to it. We have ample proof that your true calling is music, not religion. Love God to the utmost; be a good and true son; and you will then attain to the highest eminence in art, to which you have been predestined by the Almighty.

Ignaz Moscheles.

Doctors suggested a complete change of scenery and so father and son retired to Boulogne. In this salubrious setting Liszt rapidly recovered both his strength and good spirits, but with cruel irony his father became seriously ill with typhoid fever. He died in Boulogne in 1827 though not without making another vatic and remarkable utterance noted down by his dutiful son:

He said that I had a good heart and did not lack intelligence, but he feared that women would trouble my life and bring me under their sway. This provision was strange, for at that time, at the age of sixteen, I had no idea what a woman was, and in my simplicity asked my confessor to explain the sixth and ninth Commandments to me, for I was afraid I might have broken them without knowing I had done so.

Three versions of the opening of *Wilde Jagd* (Etudes d'exécution transcendante, No 8).

Ex 4

24

Chapter 2

Liszt's return to Paris and the ferment of Romanticism

Liszt's grief was bitter and intense and was shared by his mother who joined him in Paris. The death of his father, who he once affectionately described as a man of "intuitive obstinacy", exacerbated an inner emptiness and insecurity.

When death had robbed me of my father . . . and I began to foresee what art *might* be and what the artist *must* be, I felt overwhelmed by all the impossibilities which surrounded me and barred the way which my thoughts indicated as the best. Besides, finding no sympathetic word from anyone harmonizing with me in mind, either among the contented leaders of society, or, still less, among the artists who were slumbering in comfortable indifference, knowing nothing of the aims I had in view, nothing of the powers with which I felt endowed, there came over me a bitter disgust against art, such as it appeared to me: vilified and degraded to the level of a more or less profitable handicap, branded a source of amusement for distinguished society. I had sooner be anything in the world than a musician in the pay of the exalted, patronized and salaried by them like a conjuror, or the learned dog Munito. Peace to his memory!

Indeed Liszt was precipitated into such gloom and misanthropy that an obituary appeared saying, "Franz Liszt, October 22, 1811, died Paris 1828."

However, mother and son's material needs had somehow to be met and so Liszt took up teaching. "Poverty", he said, "that old mediator between man and evil, tore me from my solitude and meditation and often brought me before a public on whom not only my own but my mother's existence depended".

The Paris of the twenties and thirties was in any case heady stuff for a youth still in his teens. A grotesque social masquerade, it formed an arena where temporary attachments were made or broken as easily as exchange of partners at a ball. Small wonder that the cynical Heine

Hummel.

was able to exclaim, "when dear God is bored in heaven he opens the window and contemplates the boulevards of Paris."

It was above all a world of artists who prided themselves on being above the moral law, living evidence of the saying, 'the artist can afford to be immoral.' This *palais royale* parade was a far cry from the cloistered and contemplative life Liszt had begged for and he entered into its spirit, though with qualified musical, as opposed to social, success. His performance of his old warhorse the Hummel B minor Concerto hardly met with the customary acclaim. Writing in *La Revue Musicale* Fétis issued a sharp and significant rebuke, significant because it somehow mirrored the unsatisfactory nature of Liszt's life at this time.

What a pity that natural gifts such as those possessed by M. Liszt are employed solely to convert music into the subject for a thimble-rigger and conjuror. This is not for what this enchanting art is destined . . . Profit from

26

Caroline de Saint-Cricq (later the Countess d'Artigaux).

The Countess Adèle de Laprunarède.

time where your still-virgin faculties permit your talent to change direction; take a step back and be the first among the young pianists, and have the courage to renounce brilliant frivolities for advances that are more substantial. You will reap the rewards.

It is interesting that Fétis should accuse Liszt of the very lack of seriousness Liszt had so recently deplored.

Not surprisingly, Liszt had little difficulty in attracting the most affluent students and these included what might be called the first of his literature and philosophy ladies, Caroline de Saint Crique, the seventeen-year-old daughter of Charles X's Minister of Commerce. Like so many of Liszt's later and celebrated relationships this began with serious conversation and ended with passion, and before long Liszt, already flouting the conventions of the time, fell heavily in love. A liaison between a piano teacher and girl of noble birth was unthinkable, and Caroline's lessons, idyllically prolonged far into the night, abruptly terminated. Liszt was summoned to the Presence where thanks coldly offered preceded the word of dismissal. Caroline was packed off to a convent and within a few months was suitably and safely married to the Count d'Arigaux, a country nobleman. Liszt's adolescent passion had burned wth furious heat and it would be difficult to overestimate the slight to his feelings and to his pride. In a sense he never recovered from this romantic setback, a forcible reminder of his lowly status and an even more stinging token of the rigidity of the current social order. Outwardly snobbish and fawning he became a tireless fighter for artists' rights, retaliating with impressive savagery whenever his standing was queried. Foreshadowing E.M. Forster's belief in an aristocracy of the plucky and sensitive he was quick to assert that "to become noble is much more than to be born noble."

It will be seen from this that Liszt was ripe for rebellion. That such frustration and unhappiness should coincide with the dawn of Romanticism and the 1830 Revolution proved a happy stroke for posterity for Liszt, a true child of his time, was ready to emerge in all his vitality and novel genius. And whatever rebuffs he later suffered he never again allowed himself to sink into such a state of negation or apathy.

Snap definitions of Romanticism such as "the addition of strangeness to beauty" or "the Renaissance of Wonder" however inadequate, suggest something of the colossal ferment of energy about to rise to the surface. At all events, in the Paris of 1827 there was a growing dissatisfaction with the old order, with its rigid adherence to superficial decoration, rules and formality. For Victor Hugo there were

neither rules nor models, or rather there are not other rules than the general

Comte de Saint-Simon.

love of nature which encompass the whole art, and the special laws that for every composition result from the conditions of existence peculiar to each subject. The former are eternal, internal and remain: the latter variable, external and serve only once.

Such a creed was understandably appealing to the young Liszt and it combined with all he had learnt from the Abbé Félicité de Lamenais, a strong religious and romantic influence and the current vogue of Saint-Simonism to help him from failure to triumph. It was after all de Lamenais who saw in art a moral solution to mankind's ills and Saint-Simon who aimed "to unite the flesh and the spirit and sanctify the one by the other." There were six basic tenets in Saint-Simon's philosophy, first "to improve the quality of human life through the dissemination of scientific knowledge; secondly, to reorganize society in order that one's work, not one's birth would determine one's place in the social hierarchy; thirdly, to work for the emancipation of women; fourthly to prohibit idleness, fifthly to distribute wealth equitably, and last to 'humanize' religion.

Such a pragmatic stance was the opposite of vaguely poetic, the opposite of some Arnoldian, remotely glimpsed horizon or possibility. It was hardly a case of "wandering between two worlds, one dead/the other powerless to be born" or of a future age "more fortunate, alas! than we,/Which without hardness will be sage/And gay without frivolity." Liszt sensed immediate and irresistible realities and sympathised with both de Lamenais and Saint Simon's view of artists

. . . in the light of priests, agents of government, who by the happiness and depth of their thoughts, harmonies, pictures, sculptures, should awaken, foster and mould in the breasts of the people lasting sympathy for all that is good and noble.

This expression and evocation of emotion became the new ideal and derived less from a single and easily defined cause than from a vital and complex mutation, that of the change from public and widely held ideals to the world of private consciousness, of individualism. The individuals who asked of each aspect of the social organism, "what does it mean to *me*?" The essential quality of art would henceforth lie in its intensity rather than its formal logic or elegance, and questions rather than answers to life's profoundest dilemmas would become the order of the day. Above all it would express emotions, that "overflow of powerful feelings" so beloved of Wordsworth, and rarely could an artist have been so equipped to express musically such a philosophy than Liszt. Indeed, the ferment of activity was such that attempts to still or contradict its momentum for one moment were akin to trying to stop a turbine with a toothpick. The entire movement had an inexorable impetus and force that swept all before it.

The Abbé Félicité de Lamennais.

Victor Hugo.

It is important to realise, too, that Paris in the first half of the nineteenth century was the centre of the Romantic movement, and in this "community of exalted souls" Liszt rapidly came to embody *the* Romantic artist *par excellence*. Victor Hugo, Alfred de Musset, George Sand, Balzac, Heine, Lamartine, Théophile Gautier, Dumas, Alfred de Vigny were all ablaze with the new movement, while Delacroix, Courbet and Doumer expressed in painting a no less pronounced break with the past. Musically, Berlioz, Chopin and Paganini were to exert a powerful influence on the young, ardent and impressionable Liszt who, suddenly secure in his newly discovered awareness, found ready allies to emulate and, if necessary, excel.

Given such a stimulus and an atmosphere as charged as "a dance on a volcano" Liszt's misery vanished as if by magic and he became incessantly active. A *Symphonie Revolutionaire* was commenced but not completed and with a sudden and insatiable thirst for knowledge he started a private study programme that would have daunted all but the most hardy and enthusiastic of souls.

My mind and fingers are working like lost souls. Homer, the Bible, Lock, Byron, Hugo, Lamartine, Chateaubriand, Beethoven, Bach, Hummel, Mozart, Weber, are all about me. I study them, meditate on them, devour them furiously. In addition I work four or five hours at exercises (thirds, sixths, octaves, tremolos, repeated notes, cadenzas, etc). Ah, if only I don't go mad you will find in me an artist . . .

Alfred de Musset.

The July Revolution in Paris, 1830.

Théophile Gautier.

Alfred de Vigny.

Liszt in 1830.

This change from despair to exultancy was sufficient for Liszt to express his political feelings with a characteristic bravado. Confronted by the King, Louis Philippe (known as the 'Citizen King' on account of his superficial show of egalitarianism) Liszt replied to his assertion that much had changed with "yes, Sire, but not for the better," an insult which cost him the Legion of Honour.

At last Liszt had not only acquired a sense of context, an awareness of the vital part he could play in a new and burgeoning movement but an impetus and thrust derived from several irresistible influences. And chief of these was Paganini who appeared in Paris in 1831 and transformed Liszt's imagination and musical horizons for ever.

Eugène Delacroix.

Frederick Chopin.

The 'Revolutionary' Symphony.

Nicolo Paganini.

The 'diabolic' Paganini.

Chateaubriand.

It would be hard to overestimate the influence of this phenomenal virtuoso on the young and vividly susceptible Liszt. Almost immediately he saw the role of the virtuoso in a new light. Unworthy or superficial antics were transformed in his mind into an altogether more elevated climate of feeling. Suddenly the virtuoso was one who could cause "the spirit to speak. Then only does the virtuoso become the high priest of art, in whose warmth dead letters assume life and meaning, and whose lips reveal the secrets of art to the sons of men."

With ever-increasing zeal Liszt had no doubts concerning his future role as he continued to see the virtuoso as one

called upon to make emotion speak, and weep and sing and sigh – to bring it to life in his consciousness. He creates passions he will call to light in all their brilliance. He breathes life into the lethargic body, infuses it with fire, enlivens it with the pulse of charm and grace. He changes the earthly form into a living being, penetrating it with the spark which Prometheus snatched from Jupiter's flesh. He must send the form he has created soaring into the transparent ether; he must arm it with a thousand winged weapons; he must call up scent and blossom, and breathe the breath of life.

Hector Berlioz.

Chapter 3

Paganini, Berlioz and Chopin

A brief glance at Paganini will quickly explain Liszt's euphoria and the appeal made to the least subtle aspect of his always impressionable nature. A partial parallel between Liszt's and Paganini's early acclaim is evident, though the latter's background was coloured by a parental cruelty and opportunism mercifully unknown to Liszt.

Paganini's parents combined ruthless commercial ambition with religious hypocrisy. This led to results that were both uncannily brilliant and tragically insecure. Fiction and reality became inseparable and Paganini's constant ill-health and nervous irritability were a high price to pay for his 'success'. An apostle of the spectacular he quickly became the stuff of which dreams, and particularly commercial dreams, are made. His red and yellow clothing and blue-tinted spectacles accentuated his cadaverous appearance. People were known to cross themselves if he accidentally touched them and it was reported that his famous G string had formed part of his wife's intestines. Others, encouraged to general hysteria, saw the Devil guiding his elbow while he played, and stories of Paganini's grotesque feats became legion.

Paganini's egotism was no less boundless and he behaved with the most startling rudeness to all and sundry. His smart repartee and superficial wit in lieu of genuine intelligence were much admired and it is revealing that while Schubert earned a grand total of £575 for over a thousand compositions Paganini earned the same figure for eight concerts given during the last tragic years of Schubert's life.

The absurdity and vulgarity of the age were somehow crystallized by such blatant sensationalism and injustice. While Schubert lay forgotten, gloves were worn *à la Paganini* and only the rival attraction of a recently acquired giraffe at the zoo caused Paganini to cancel a concert. Like the yo-yo or hoolahoop the violin became the latest craze and leaders of fashion and society quickly forsook their samplers and needlework for more strenuous activity. Even Rossini

Rossini.

claimed that Paganini's playing was one of three events in his otherwise genial life which had caused him to weep, the others being the failure of his first opera and, the loss of a turkey stuffed with truffles which accidentally fell overboard during a boat ride.

But beneath the façade was an often wretchedly sick man. Even the refined cruelty which Paganini was capable of on occasion becomes forgiveable when we read his famous diary which reads, "*purgativo, riposo, purgativo, vomi-purga, vomitivo, purgativo* etc." over a period of nine days. It is also revealing to find Paganini's compositions defined in one modern dictionary of music as "lacking in emotional depth," and in another as "thin and commonplace". The sad but tangible evidence of the inner man is a heavy qualification of a virtuoso whose success was dwarfed only by his excess. The twenty-four *Caprices* are a *bête-noir* of perennial fascination for intrepid violinists, but the *Moto Perpetuo*, with its legendary quantity of notes, and the Concertos have only tarnished with the years.

Schubert.

Rossini.

Paganini.

Liszt, knowing his own superiority as a composer, quickly realised that he could write works for the piano which equalled Paganini's diablerie but which excelled it in musical depth and substance. The first fruits, then, of this new and decisive influence were not surprisingly the *Six Grandes Études de Paganini* which were completed in 1837 (extensively polished and revised in 1851), one year before the picturesque brilliance of the *Two Études de Concert*, *Waldesrauschen* and *Gnomenreigen*, and three years before the Twelve *Études d'exécution transcendante*. Here, essentially violinistic effects, the skips of *La Campanella* or the *sautillé* bowing in the arpeggios of No. 4 are dazzlingly transformed into pianistic splendour and beauty. These works, together with the Faust Symphony, the B minor Sonata, the Dante Symphony, the *Totentanz, Ab Irato* Etude, Mephisto Waltzes and Polka etc. to name but a few, are all remarkable instances of 'terribilita' (where the music's natural substance is spiced and intensified by a macabre and melodramatic element). This, combined with a phenomenal quality which delights in its own excess and exuberance, and which is captured to a certain extent in the Italian word, 'sprezzatura', can be heard to a greater or lesser degree in all these works. And we need to use our historical imagination if we are to realise fully the impact of, say, the *Grande Fantasie sur la Clochette* (later greatly clarified and refined to become the more familiar *La Campanella*). The daemonic influence of Paganini was greatly increased by the transferrence of devices considered the exclusive province of the violinist. Today, we take the brilliant execution of cascades of octaves and repeated notes for granted, but in their time such difficulties were considered virtually impossible, even allowing for the greatly increased facility possible on the new pianos of the period.

And here, surely, lay the foundation of music of a subsequent generation, such as Ravel's *Gaspard de la Nuit* where such period diablerie is eerily changed into something undreamed of even by Liszt. It is, incidentally, important to realise that Liszt later repudiated Paganini's influence and in 1840 pleaded with all artists of the future to

. . . gladly and readily decline to play the conceited and egotistical role which we hope has had in Paganini its last brilliant representative. May he set his goal within, and not outside, himself, and be the means of virtuosity, and not its end. May he constantly keep in mind that, though the saying is *Noblesse oblige*, in a far higher degree than nobility – *Genie oblige*!

A powerful if less immediate influence was provided by Berlioz. As live as an electric eel under Paganini's saturnine spell, Liszt's nature ricocheted in another direction under the impact of Berlioz's *Symphonie Fantastique* when he attended the first performance of this

Berlioz.

momentous work in Paris in 1832. Here, surely, was the symphony Liszt had planned but failed to complete and few works could have expressed the Romantic upheaval of the times more decisively. Liszt was overwhelmed, and at once transcribed the entire score for the piano on the night of the concert, refining and completing his work the following year.

Berlioz and Liszt were soul mates, rebels and pioneers who were exalted and contemptuous of rules and general propriety. Their partnership in Beethoven's 'Emperor' Concerto in Paris in 1841 must have been unforgettable.

Then there was Chopin, a sobering influence, whose exclusive and irreproachable genius pulled Liszt up in his tracks. Drunk with the vistas opened up by Paganini he was now deflected by an altogether more inward and poetic quality, by a more settled and single-minded composer whose direction, unlike Liszt's, was unfaltering from start to finish. As Schumann wrote, "it appears as if the sight of Chopin brought Liszt to his senses" and momentarily halted in its zig-zag course his reeling punch drunk brilliance. Reflecting on this new and quietly formidable genius he wrote,

to our endeavours, to our struggles, first the standing so much in need of certainty, being met as it were at that time by wiseacres who shook their heads at us, rather than by glorious opponents, he lent us that support of a calm, unshakeable conviction, equally armed to resist flagging or allurement.

Of Chopin's ornamentation he exclaimed,

this kind of ornament, the type of which had previously only been found in the fioritura of the old great school of Italian singing, received from Chopin the unexpected and the manifold that lies beyond the power of the human voice; whereas until then the latter alone had been slavishly copied with ornaments that had become stereotypes and monotonous, Chopin united those wonderous harmonious progressions which lent a dignified and serious character to passages which from their highest nature of the subject, lay no claim to any deep significance.

Liszt retained a life-long admiration for Chopin's playing and in one of his celebrated master-classes given so many years later he said,

such a poetic temperament as Chopin's never existed, nor have I heard such delicacy and refinement of playing. The tone, though small, was absolutely beyond criticism and although his execution was not forcible, nor by any means fitted for the concert room, still it was perfect in the extreme.

Liszt later wrote his *Life of Chopin* in Weimar in 1849 but, some characteristically individual insights apart, that most effusive work (the opening, "Chopin, sweet and harmonious genius" sets the general tone) tells us less than the above comments. Here, for example, is his description of that curiously untranslatable Polish word, *zal*.

Zal! Strange word embracing a strange diversity and a strange philosophy! Susceptible of different interpretations, it includes within itself all the deep humility of a regret born of resignation and without murmuring, whilst bowing before the stern fiat of necessity and the inscrutable decrees of Providence; but changing its character as soon as it is spoken to man, and assuming an indirect meaning, it signifies agitation, excitement, rancour, revolt, filled with reproach, vengeance, premeditated, never-ceasing menace and threatening retaliation ever becomes possible and meanwhile feeding itself upon a bitter if fruitless hatred.

It is relevant, too, to realise that Liszt's open admiration for Chopin was tinged with uneasiness. Chilling and exclusive when provoked, Chopin may have sat open-mouthed and even a trifle piqued at Liszt's piano playing ("I write to you without knowing what my pen is scribbling because at this moment Liszt is playing my Studies and transporting me outside of respectable thought. I should like to steal from him the way to play my own Studies.") He was referring to the opus 10 Studies dedicated to Liszt, but he was much less impressed by Liszt's own compositions; clearly for him the outpouring of a facile and inferior talent.

When I think of Liszt as a creative artist, he appears before my eyes rouged, on stilts, and blowing into Jericho trumpets *fortissimo* and *pianissimo* – or I see him dicoursing on art, on the nature of creativeness and how one should create. Yet as a creator he is an ass. He knows everything better than anyone. He wants to attain Parnassus on another man's Pegasus. This is *entre nous* – he is an excellent binder who puts other people's works between his covers . . . I still say that he is a clever craftsman without a vestige of talent . . .

Liszt's lifelong devotion, then, went coldly unrequited though it is only fair to add that his mature works were written long after Chopin's death in 1849 and it is hardly an exaggeration to say that Chopin could scarcely have known, let alone considered, Liszt seriously as a composer. Liszt was also aware of Chopin's attitude and while his egotism was undoubtedly bruised his admiration remained intact. This expressed itself after Chopin's death in a curious posthumous identification with Chopin's musical spirit. His *Funéraille, Berceuse,* the two Polonaises and two Ballades (the second of which is nicely differentiated from Chopin's by Sacheverell Sitwell as "concerned more with epic than personal feeling; cities in flames" etc.) are particular instances, and the subtle and unmistakeable influence is there again in works such as *Les Cloches de Genève (Années de Pèlerinage*, Book 1 Switzerland, whether in the 1835 version or the dramatic revision of 1850) or the Three Concert Studies. In the latter the Chopinesque bias is suggested in their alternative picturesque title, *Trois Caprices Poetiques* and the delicate chromatic whirlwind of *La Leggierezze*, the second of the three studies, a work not unrelated to the first of Chopin's *Trois Nouvelles Études*, also in F minor. There is evidence, too, for seeing Liszt's Tenth Transcendental Study in F minor as a natural if very Lisztian consequence of Chopin's F minor study from opus 10 (music dedicated to Liszt).

Yet even if we hear once more "the hoof beats of the Polish cavalry" in the central octave uproar of *Funérailles* and recall Chopin's unchanging left hand pattern in the *Berceuse*, the rhetorical grandeur and decorative ardour of these respective works are wholly Liszt's.

In brief, it took an extensive amount of cross-pollination for Liszt to find his own voice and poetic identity; a simple fact unknown to Chopin who would doubtless have seen Liszt's 'tribute' once more as the work of "an excellent binder who puts other people's works between his covers . . ."

Chopin (from the famous portrait by Delacroix).

Chapter 4

Marie d'Agoult

In 1833 an influence of another kind appeared. A party given at Chopin's Paris apartment included a dazzling assortment of guests; Liszt, Berlioz, Heine, Meyerbeer, Mickiewicz, George Sand, Delacroix – and the Countess Marie d'Agoult attended. Marie d'Agoult was born in 1805, the daughter of a French emigré, the Vicomte de Flavigny. Described by one writer as "six inches of snow covering twenty feet of lava" this formidable woman's romantic notions of Bohemian life outside the limiting social circle she attended was satisfied in no uncertain terms by her meeting with Liszt.

... the door opened, and a wonderful apparition – for I can find no other word to describe the most extraordinary man I have ever seen, entered. He possessed a tall and extremely slender figure, a pallid face with big eyes of the deepest sea-green that flashed fire, a suffering but strong cast of features, a gliding step that seemed to float along the ground rather than tread firmly upon it, and a distracted and restless expression like that of a phantom for whom the hour when it must return to darkness is about to sound. Thus did I see before me this young genius, whose entire life aroused at that time as much curiosity as his triumphs had once exacted envy.

Heinrich Heine.

Marie's response to Liszt's charisma was not without precedent. Already in 1828 Wilhelm von Lenz had written of Liszt's "unspeakably attractive features" and his smile which "was like the glitter of a dagger in sunlight."

Perhaps Marie had been reading Coleridge and saw in Liszt a reincarnation of the protagonist of "Kubla Khan" (published in 1816), and was at once attracted to a figure dangerous and appealing to her essentially masochistic nature enthralled by so dangerous a figure. "And all should cry Beware! Beware! /His flashing eyes, his floating hair!/Weave a circle round him thrice,/And close your eyes with holy dread,/For he on honey-dew hath fed,/And drunk the milk of Paradise."

Marie d'Agoult.

Liszt in 1832.

Marie aroused a scarcely less positive response in Liszt. For both it was love at first sight, though love tinted by ulterior motives. For, once she perceived the extent of Liszt's fascination for her high-born beauty, Marie saw the possibility of a glorious escape from her privileged but limited salon success. Desperate for freedom she was willing to form a socially unacceptable liaison and indeed scandalous alliance and replace her security with her husband – the dull if respectable Count Charles d'Agoult – with the dubious reward of

Title page of *Chapelle de Guillaume Tell (Années de pèlerinage,* Book 1, Suisse).

being the mistress of a volatile and notoriously fickle genius, his *femme inspiratrice*. Her plan was both clear and tenacious. It was also as familiar as it was naïve. She would appeal to Liszt's better self and woo him away from his superficial success and aplomb. With her to guide him he would relinquish his temporary brilliance as a performer and achieve permanent glory as a composer. So great was their love that they would need nothing else and live in glorious seclusion shielded from the rabble, the world's cruelties and demands. There would, of course, be no other woman for competition or even temporary diversion.

Such a romantic or unrealistic notion stemmed from Marie's instability. Depression and psychosomatic illness had already led to her breakdown. Difficult and neurotic she confessed that since her wedding day "she had not enjoyed a single happy hour". Later, involved in an altogether more impassioned relationship she wrote, "sometimes I am afraid that I am going mad, my brain is tired . . . "

Alas, Marie, a writer of uncertain talent, underestimated Liszt's needs and nature, the demands of a genius of limitless force and range.

Liszt

Liszt, at the time of his meeting with Marie d'Agoult.

George Sand.

Liszt was also much too pragmatic in his approach to love to miss the opportunities offered by such an alliance. Socially he had everything to gain while Marie had everything to lose. Dragging her down the social ladder he ascended with such speed he attached himself to an outwardly attractive situation with chameleon-like facility. The man who said that no earthly passion would ever take possession of him now exclaimed,

I feel as if I had never loved before, never been loved! My God, my God, never let us be separated, have pity on us! . . . Oh, God, thanks and benediction of God be on you . . . Live only in you, absorbed and almost deified by you . . . You have been, you are noble and grand and sublime . . . You make me very proud.

Later he advises moderation, realising that it is Marie who is being put to the test, but then, swept away by his rhetorical passion of the moment exclaims,

Marie! Marie! Oh let me repeat that name a hundred times, a thousand times. For three days it has lived within me, oppressed me, burned me . . . Eternity in your arms . . . Heaven, hell, all, all in you, and again in you . . . Oh, let me be mad, insane . . . Common, prudent, narrow reality no longer suffices for me; we must live with all our life, all our love, all our woes! You believe me capable, do you not, of sacrifice, of virtue, of moderation, of religion? . . . This is to be, to be! The day when you can say to me with all your soul, all your heart, all your mind, 'Franz, let us blot out, forget, forgive for ever, everything that has been incomplete, distressing and perhaps wretched in the past; let us be all in all to each other, for now I understand you and pardon you as I love you – that day – and may it be soon – we will fly far from the world; we will live, love and die for each other alone.

Within a remarkably short time the *liaison dangereuse* became an open affair, surveyed by Marie's friends with appalled fascination. However, impervious to their pleas she fled with Liszt to Geneva which although described as "a place of anointed Calvinism" made her less conscious of prying eyes and condemnation. Liszt and Marie at once established a Bohemian *ménage* that attracted the attention of George Sand who, unlike some others, took a broad view of their romantic and daring alliance.

In Geneva Liszt wrote the first book of his *Années de Pèlerinage*, music picturesquely evocative of Swiss legends, alpine stream, storms, and the bells of Geneva itself. In his preface to the first edition he wrote,

Having recently visited many new countries, many diverse cities, many spots consecrated by history and poetry: having felt that the varied aspects of Nature of the scenes attached thereunto did not pass before my eyes in vain

Etienne de Sénancour.

Title page of Au Lac de Wallenstadt (*Années de pèlerinage*, Book 1, Suisse).

pictures, but that they stirred upon my soul deep emotions; that there was established between them and myself a vague but immediate relationship, an indefinite but real connection, an inexplicable but certain communication, I have tried to express in music a few of the strongest of my sensations, of my most vivid perceptions . . . As instrumental music progresses, develops, frees itself from first fetters, it tends to become more and more imbued with that ideality which has marked the perfection of the plastic arts, to become not only a simple combination of sounds, but a poetic language more apt perhaps than poetry itself to express all that within us oversteps the accustomed horizon, everything that escapes analysis, everything that attracts itself inaccessible depths, imperishable denisons, infinite presentiments. It is in this connection, with this tendency that I have undertaken the work published today, addressing myself to a few rather than the crowd; deserving not success but the suffrage of the small number of those who conceive of art a destination other than that of applauding a pastime during a few idle hours, and ask more of it than the futile distraction of a passing amusement.

On a more specifically literary level *Vallée d'Obermann* was composed under the influence of Etienne Pivert de Sénancour, whose speculative and pessimistic works fired the imagination of all those suffering from what was called *le maladie du siècle*. In de Sénancour's work the questions, *que veux je?* and *que demande à la nature?* haunt the text with their plaintive and dramatic repetitions.

Marie was, of course, entranced. This was just the sort of musical-poetic 'honeymoon' she had envisaged and, with a characteristically literary turn of phrase, she heard "a melancholy harmony, imitative

Liszt in 1837.

Title page of Pastorale
(*Années de pèlerinage*,
Book 1, Suisse).

of the sighs of waves and the cadence of oars" in the pellucid, dancing waters of *Au lac de Wallenstadt*. For Marie

ramparts of granite, inaccessible mountains now arose between ourselves and the world as if to conceal us in those deep valleys, among the shadowy pines, where the only sound was the murmuring of waterfalls

Geneva may have seemed boorish and provincial after the glitter of Paris but initially it proved more than satisfactory. Liszt founded a

Conservatorium of Music and his assessments of his students (invariably women) range from "vicious technique (if technique there be)" to "beautiful eyes." There was also a memorable trip to Chamonix in the company of George Sand who surveyed her friend's relationship with an amused if far from disinterested condescension. In authentic Byronic style Liszt registered at the hotel as "a musician philosopher, born in Parnassus, coming from Doubt and journeying towards Truth", and together with his companions alarmed the other guests with his extravagant and noisy behaviour.

Liszt's roving eye and insatiable energy were momentarily stilled, but not for long. A chill shadow fell slowly but inexorably over the Geneva idyll, and Liszt began to chafe against the restraints imposed

Byron.

The Inn at Chamonix.

Sigismond Thalberg.

Princess Belgiojoso.

on his free spirit. Longing for the old excitements, or "puerile agitation", – to use his own phrase – he overcame Marie's protests. Rumours of a pianist who could rival his supposedly unique virtuosity had reached him from Paris where Sigismond Thalberg (born in 1812) now held musical court and sway. This new idol of aristocratic birth could supposedly imitate the sound of three rather than two hands and "realise the Zen ideal of central peace with peripheral combat." He was, further, a composer of distinction.

Liszt was undoubtedly piqued and journeyed to Paris with a savage glitter in his eye. Writing in the *Gazette Musicale* he discussed this latest phenomenon with an elaborate show of civility before embarking on a crescendo of abuse. Thalberg's actual works he found "so empty, so mediocre", his playing as profound as the diamond studs so ostentatiously worn on his shirt. Later he swept Thalberg's challenge and performance into oblivion in an even more decisive manner. Thalberg played his own Fantasie on *God Save The King* and *Moses Fantasy* before an audience of four hundred. Liszt played Weber's *Konzertstücke*, Beethoven's *Hammerklavier* Sonata (Liszt was a tireless propagandist for Beethoven and very possibly his foremost interpreter) and his own *Niobe Fantasy* before an audience of four thousand at the Opera House. To cap it all both pianists were invited to perform at a gladiatorial soirée, a sort of foretaste of today's ubiquitous competitions. This was given by the Princess Cristina Belgiojoso, a lady notorious both for her amorous and political intrigues, and it was announced, "the greatest interest . . . will be without question the simultaneous appearance of two talents whose rivalry at this time agitated the musical world and is like the indecisive balance between Rome and Carthage. Liszt and Thalberg will take turns at the piano".

The outcome of this flamboyant affair (viewed with distate from afar by Marie) was unanimous. Thalberg was the first pianist in the world, but Liszt the *only* one. The matter was settled once and for all and as Thalberg retreated in shame Liszt returned to Geneva in triumph.

A well earned break at Nohant with George Sand followed but was not a success. Two such strong-willed women as George Sand and Marie d'Agoult were unlikely to exist in a state of amity for long and Marie's agitation increased when she noted the predictable effect of Liszt's piano playing on their host.

When Franz Liszt plays I am comforted. All my sorrows are exalted, I love those broken phrases that he flings on the piano and which remain half in the air. The leaves of the Linden finish the melody for me. Mighty artist, sublime in great things, always sublime in small ones, and yet sad, gnawed by a secret wound. Fortunate man, loved by a beautiful woman, intelligent and chaste . . . what do you lack, miserable ingrate! Ah! if only I were loved . . !

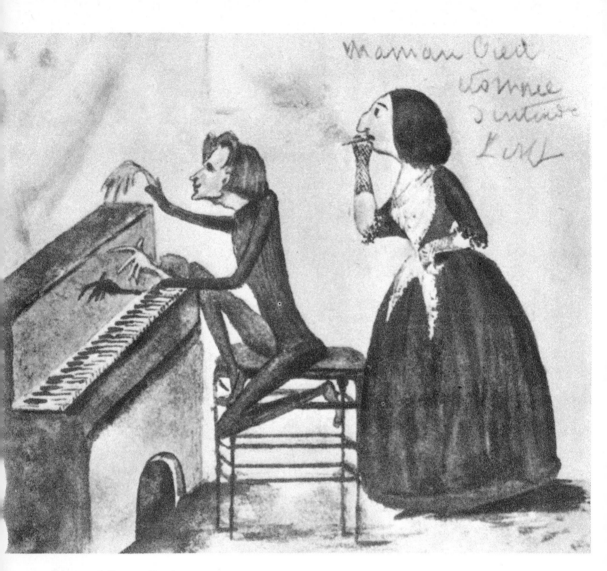

Liszt and George Sand.

George Sand's mischief-making propensity was already alerted and so Marie retreated to Italy with Liszt. For the moment Liszt was happy to succumb, agreeing with his mistress that "work, contemplation, love and solitude – or at any rate solitude *à deux* – were the only necessities for true fulfilment. Writing in her journal Marie exclaimed in wonder over their new found happiness.

I am astonished to find him so constantly gay, so happy in the absolute solitude in which we are living. At any age when everything impels a man towards outer activity, when movement and change are almost a condition of existence, he, whose mind is so communicative, he, whose occupations have always taken him into the world, he, the artist, that is to say the man of sympathies, of emotion, of imagination, concentrates all his faculties within

50

George Sand (portrait by Delacroix).

the narrow frame of life *tête-à-tête*. A bad piano, a few books, the conversation of a serious woman, suffice for him. He renounces all the joys of *amour-propre*, the excitement of combat, the amusements of social life, even the delight of being useful and doing good; he renounces them all without even appearing to be conscious that he is renouncing.

All this came as a relief after Liszt's previous return to his old bad ways, a return, however, reinforced by Marie's peculiar sense of estrangement. Successful as she was at capturing Liszt's outer self, his inner domain proved frustratingly beyond even her tentacular grasp. Sitting invisible to the audience at one of Liszt's concerts, aware of her unsatisfactory social position in the eyes of a notably conservative and provincial society, she became conscious of another more subtle form of alienation. Catching Liszt's eye as he commenced one of his concerts as he ensnared his audience with his every gesture, she says:

How can I describe what I felt. It was Franz I saw, and yet it was not Franz. It was as if someone were impersonating him on the stage, with great art except the facial resemblance. And his playing disturbed me. His prodigious, brilliant, incomparable virtuosity was indeed there, but I felt it nevertheless as something alien to me. Where were we? Was I dreaming? Was I the victim of a delirium? Who had taken me there? For what purpose? I felt an inexpressible anguish. From that day a change was wrought in my existence; it brought with it a new and difficult trial of my courage.

George Sand's home at Nohant.

The Flood of Pest.

Rarely can anyone have captured more tellingly this particular and painful dilemma. Within a few sentences and frantic rhetorical questions Marie sees and conveys her true situation, namely that the virtuoso or 'egotistical sublime' in Liszt could never be permanently held in check or constrained by her, or, indeed, by anyone else.

However, Italy gave her a breathing space. A second daughter, Cosima, was born in Como in 1837 (the first, Blandine, had been born in Geneva two years earlier) and there, under the inspiration of the Italian painters and writers Liszt and Marie loved best, the second book of the *Années de Pèlerinage* was begun, though not completed until 1849. The tributes to Raphael and Dante (*Spozalizio* and *Après une lecture du Dante*) in particular show Liszt at the height of his creative strength; grand, eloquent, introspective and already (notably

52

'The Thinker' (Michelangeli) the inspiration for *Il Penseroso* (*Anneés de pèlerinage*, Book 2, Italy).

'The Betrothal of the Virgin' (Raphael), the inspiration for *Sposalizio* (*Années de pèlerinage, Book 2, Italie*).

in the darkly meditative *Il Pensieroso*, inspired by Michelangelo's '*The Thinker*', in the Church of San Lorenzo, Florence) alive with glowing and novel harmonies so suggestive of his future work. The Three Petrach Sonnets, too, whether in their vocal or piano settings, recreate the poet's ardour in a wholly unforgettable way.

But such domestic contentment was as short-lived as it was inadequate and the damage and distress incurred by the Danube flood of 1838 provided the necessary impetus for one of Liszt's characteristically mixed gestures. His generosity was undeniable but so was his opportunism, and his concern for the victims of the disaster blended uneasily with letters to Geneva telling of the greatest personal triumphs, of his brilliance and personal magnetism. Liszt was rarely a complete altruist and so once more Marie's dream of romantic seclusion was threatened not only by tales of social advances on the grandest scale and of the dreaded theatrical aplomb, but with other even less acceptable diversions. There were reminders, too, of the maxim that "doing good for some public reward is not doing good; it is doing something for public reward. That it also does good may seem to be its justification, but it is a dangerous justification." At all events Marie's response was bitter and disillusioned.

Liszt.

The way in which he spoke about his stay in Vienna brought me down from the clouds. They had found armorial bearings for him – He wanted me to be heroic. The women had thrown themselves at his head; he was no longer embarrassed over his lapses. He reasoned about them like a philosopher. He spoke of necessities . . . He was elegantly dressed; his talk was about nothing but princes; he was secretly pleased with his exploits as Don Juan. One day I said something that hurt him; I called him a *Don Juan parvenu*. I summoned up my pride as a woman, as a *grande dame*, as a republican, to judge him from above. He had made money easily; he had left it for the victims of the floods; but he had realised that in two years he could make a fortune.

There is a disconcerting baldness about Liszt's manner and behaviour at this time. Although it is simplistic to speak of him as nothing more than an "aggressive arrivist reeking of vulgarity", or, as Heine has it, "the very childish child of his age", it is surely true to say

Alphonsine Duplessis (La Dame aux Camélias).

An evening with Liszt. Distinguished guests include Marie d'Agoult, George Sand, Victor Hugo, Paganini and Rossini. The scene is completed by a bust of Beethoven and a portrait of Byron.

Liszt in Hungarian costume, 1838.

that Liszt's worst instincts surfaced by way of reaction to his prolonged confinement, to the way his wings had been clipped in an increasingly one-sided relationship.

Carried away and flushed by success he brutally regaled Marie with long lists of the nobility who attended his banquets (scarcely one without a title), acknowledged applause "in the style of a king" and all because *genius oblige!* He advises Marie to exploit her aristocratic title to the full if she wishes for a success comparable to his own, adding, "being nobody, it is necessary for me to be somebody."

It was no less typical of Liszt at this time to tell Marie that they might settle romantically together, perhaps in Hungary or in Constantinople. It was also no less typical of him to write to her in 1847 telling her after the death of his former mistress, Marie Duplessis (the celebrated *La Dame aux Camélias*),

"I have told you what a singular attachment I entertained for this lovely creature when I was last in Paris. I told her I would take her with me to Constantinople . . . and now she is dead. And I know not of what strange chord of our antic elegy vibrates in my heart when I remember her, a remarkable case of *plus ça change, plus c'est la même chose*".

Cartoon sequence of
Liszt as the ultimate
virtuoso.

Liszt, 1839.

Marie now knew the complete disillusion which follows when an
idealised person suddenly becomes cruel and exploits to the full the
vulnerability of the person in love. Stung to the quick she at last
retaliated. Her accusation, "you are as sublime and as hard as Alpine
granite" gave way to her dignified assertion that she had no objection
to being his mistress but she would not be one of his mistresses. Was it
for this that she had sacrificed her position and well being? With
burning clarity she once more saw Liszt as "a charming good-for-
nothing . . . half mountebank, half juggler, who makes ideas and
sentiments disappear up his sleeve and looks complacently at the
bewildered public that applauds him". Here is proof indeed that there
is "no rage like love to hatred turned, nor hell to fury like a woman
scorned".

From then on things were never the same between Liszt and Marie,
and despite a temporary reconciliation the relationship could only go
from bad to worse. Their idyll on the Rhine island of Nonnenwerth,
which commenced in 1841, was soon interrupted. Marie's company, a
half ruined convent, a chapel and a few fishermen's huts provided
only a very temporary answer to Liszt's romantic longings, and their
grand passion terminated (together with the lease of the island) in 1842.
For Marie, Nonnenwerth was "the tomb of my dreams, of my ideals,
the remains of my hopes".

The years 1839-47 (the so-called *glanz* or glitter period) were the
acme of Liszt's career as possibly the most prodigious of all pianists
and there was only limited space among so many accumulated
triumphs for Marie.

Between 1841-2 Liszt gave over twenty concerts in Berlin.
Rellstab, a savage and inflexible critic who dipped his pen in vitriol at
the mention of Chopin wrote,

he lives the piece of music he is playing. With astonishing prowess he can
accomplish every technical feat which has previously been carried out singly
by his predecessors, as well as treating us to a complete cornucopia of new
discoveries, completely unknown effects and technical combinations,
surpassing all expectations and demand. But by far the most attractive,

captivating and stimulating element in his art is the particular spirit which he breathes into these wonderful forms.

Rellstab was himself echoing Liszt's own dazzling estimate of the true virtuoso's art and he later wrote no less ecstatically of Liszt's departure from Berlin. "He marched not *like* a King, but *as* a King surrounded with a rejoicing crowd, a King in the imperishable kingdom of the Spirit."

In 1842 Liszt's first Russian tour prompted a similar adulation and many of his admirers became delirious and inarticulate after his concerts. Thus "I left the concert hall two hours ago and am still beside myself. Where am I? Where are we? Is this reality or a dream? Did I really hear Liszt?" Lisztomania had begun in earnest.

Liszt himself took a less ecstatic view of his being a celebrity exclaiming, "always concerts! Always the servant of the public no matter what . . . no peace by day or night . . ." a lament later echoed by Anton Rubinstein and the American virtuoso Louis Morreau Gottschalk.

But the public was insatiable and earlier in 1841 Heine wrote, "all pianists pale beside him with the exception of the one and only Chopin, the Raphael of the piano. Indeed, with this one exception, all other pianists heard this year are only pianists who excel by their ability to handle their instrument. With Liszt, however, we no longer think of the conquest of difficulties – the piano vanishes and – the music appears."

Liszt's tours also included Portugal and Spain where he described Madrid, Seville, Cordoba and Granada in memorable style – "those wonderful towns in which the historic intermixture of Latin and Moorish cultures is set against an all but tropical landscape, peopled by fiery men and women of the turbulent south".

For Liszt, Seville Cathedral was ". . . an epic in granite, an architectural symphony whose eternal chords vibrate in the infinite".

It was during this period that one superlative estimate of Liszt's playing followed another, tributes later fragmented and distorted with no less devotion by his enemies, his satirists and caricaturists.

57

Liszt (Ingres), 1839.

Chapter 5

Escape from Marie

A third child was born to Marie in Rome in 1839. At this time Liszt's extraordinary beauty was perpetuated by Ingres who inscribed his famous portrait to Marie, a bitter-sweet tribute given the climate of her relationship with Liszt at the time.

Once again news of a projected memorial to Beethoven in Bonn and the lack of funds needed for its completion gave Liszt both an ideal excuse and an opportunity to express his admiration for Beethoven:

. . . For us musicians, Beethoven's work is like the pillar of cloud and fire which guided the Israelites through the desert – a pillar of cloud to guide us by day, a pillar of fire to guide us by night, "so that we may progress both day and night."

But Liszt escaped from one form of disturbance to another, for the Bonn celebrations were marred from the start by ill-feeling. Liszt arrived with his mistress of the moment, Lola Montez, and in a final banquet accidentally omitted all reference to the French who were present and who had contributed to the fund. The dinner concluded in an uproar and a festival created to commemorate the greatness of Beethoven degenerated into a sordid squabble. Significantly in 1870 at the centenary of Beethoven's birth Liszt was not invited and was replaced by Hiller.

Nonetheless Liszt scored his usual personal triumph and achieved a glorious *réclame* in Vienna. Gone were the misgivings of his early years, his scorn for the virtuoso's shallow appeal, for the condescension of the nobility. Worshipping what he had formerly despised Liszt wrote to tell Marie of the plans by the Hungarian aristocracy to give him letters of nobility.

But although Liszt had become a "shining star" for the entire Hungarian nation these plans were rejected. Liszt had recently played the 'Rákóczy march' in Pressberg, fanning the flames of unrest

Lola Montez.

in the national struggle against Austria. However, there was rich compensation in a jewelled sword of honour. At its presentation Liszt, not forgetting the doctrines of Lamenais and Saint-Simon, spoke with all his customary eloquence:

... This sword, once used so heroically in defence of our country, has in this air been given into frail and peaceable hands. Is it not a symbol? Is it not to say gentlemen, that Hungary, having covered herself with glory on so many battlefields, now calls on the arts, on literature, on the sciences, all partisans of peace, to provide new examples? Is it not to say that those who toil with their minds and their hands also have a noble task, a high vision to fulfil amongst you?

Nonetheless, despite such lofty rhetoric Liszt's success was accentuated by the obviousness of his recital programmes (alive with this paraphrase and that, the Hexameron Variations, the *Grand Galop Chromatique*) though it should be added that music of a far greater simplicity and economy, such as the Six Consolations, also date from this time. However, there was nothing simple about Liszt's retinue. Fêted and applauded to an unprecedented degree his arrival in Budapest provided an excuse for Hungary once more to honour her most distinguished son. Liszt's 'Hungarian' celebrity, emphasised by

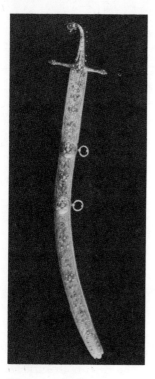

The sword of honour given to Liszt in Budapest in 1840.

Liszt.

A morning concert attended by Czerny and Berlioz, among others.

an elaborate national costume created specially for the occasion, may have been marred by his inability to speak the language (he replied to each eulogy in French) but the effect was all that could be desired.

Later, a royal command concert before Queen Victoria at Windsor could have been tarnished by the presence of Marie but, ignominiously kept like Rochester's wife from public view, her persistent presence failed to deflect attention from Liszt's success. He scored a personal triumph with Lady Blessington who, enraptured by his appearance, felt that he was wasted as a pianist. A provincial tour and some appearances in Ireland were less successful where unsophisticated audiences wondered at his shoulder length hair and grew restive during the more serious offerings. In Dublin "he played a piece, 'Sonata of Beethoven' twenty minutes long! t'was dreadful!" commented one of his concert colleagues ruefully. However, success in Copenhagen, Constantinople, Poland and Russia was unquestionable and his celebrated three hundred and sixty neckties and royal caravan (a retinue, *toute une caravane aristocratique* predating Paderewski's royal train) aroused awe and amusement wherever it travelled.

That such obvious showmanship should also arouse suspicion and enmity was no less inevitable and Liszt attracted the attention of the most gifted satirists and novelists of the day. As early as 1835 Henry Reeves described a singular instance of Liszt's charisma as follows:

61

... As the closing strains began I saw Liszt's countenance assume that agony of expression, mingled with radiant smiles of joy, which I never saw in any other human face except in paintings of our Saviour by some of the early masters; his hands rushed over the keys, the floor on which I sat shook like a wire, and the whole audience were wrapped in sound, when the hand frame of the artist gave way. He fainted in the arms of a friend who was turning over the pages for him and we bore him out in a strong fit of hysterics. The effect of this scene was really dreadful. The whole room sat breathless with fear, till Hiller came forward and announced that Liszt was already restored to consciousness and was comparatively well again. As I handed Madame de Circourt to her carriage we both trembled like poplar leaves, and I tremble scarcely less as I write this!

This scene has a strange and unnerving verisimilitude but the opening provided was irresistible.

Liszt as St Francis suffering child prodigies to come unto him.

Szt. Liszt Ferencz. Engedjétek hozzám jönni a csodagyermekeket, mert övék a jövő zenéjének országa.

Liszt as St Francis on the waves.

A certain great pianist who is as clever a manager as he is an admirable executant, pays women at the rate of twenty-five francs per concert to pretend to faint away with pleasure in the middle of a fantasia taken at such a rapid pace that it would have been humanly impossible to finish it. The pianist abruptly leaves his instrument to rush to the assistance of the poor fainting lady, while everybody in the room believes that but for this interruption the prodigious pianist would have completed the greatest of miracles. It happened one night that a woman paid to faint forgot her cue and fell fast asleep. The pianist was playing Weber's *Konzertstücke*. Relying on the lady to faint during the finale he took it at an impossible speed. What could he do in such awkward circumstances?

Stumble and bungle like an ordinary vulgar pianist, or pretend that his memory had failed him; No: he simply played the part where the faintress (excuse the word) should have taken her cue, and then fainted away himself. People crowded round the pianist, who had become a double phenomenon through his electric execution and his frail and susceptible constitution. He was carried out to the green-room. The men applauded as if they intended to bring down the ceiling; the women waved their hankerchiefs to show their enthusiasm and the faintress, on waking, fainted, perhaps really with despair at not having pretended to faint.

Balzac, too, was quick off the mark and in his novel *Beatrix* the true

63

identity of the singer, Conti, is unmistakable. Sketching the type he says,

There are men, of whom I have spoken to you, who are charlatans on the surface but honest. Such men lie to themselves. Perched on stilts they fancy that they are on their feet, and play their tricks with a sort of innocence; their vanity is in their blood; they are born actors . . . grotesquely funny like a Chinese jar; they might even laugh at themselves. Their personal impulses are generous . . . they attract danger.

He carries you up to Heaven by a song that seems to be some mysterious fluid, flowing with love; gives you a glance of ecstasy; but he keeps an eye on your admiration; he is asking himself, 'Am I really a god to these people?' And in the same instance he is perhaps saying to himself, 'I have eaten too much macaroni' . . . He is insatiable for applause; can act joy as well as grief, and he succeeds to perfection. He can please, he is loved, he can get admiration whenever he chooses.

Mendelssohn.

Liszt as St Francis
surrounded by female
admirers.

Liszt's sword of honour had already attracted attention, prompting the following verse:

"Liszt alone, of all warriors, is without reproach
For in spite of his big sword, we know that this
Has vanquished only semi-quavers
And slain only pianos."

Among the cognoscenti Liszt provoked more criticism than praise. Everyone was initially dazzled but a cooler, more detached and far from complimentary view usually followed. Mendelssohn was irritated by the "pranks he played with other people's music" though as usual Liszt had an answer to such comments.

Do you know whence comes this misunderstanding of my works? From Leipzig! You know that Mendelssohn who was the most jealous musician that ever lived always disliked me, and on one occasion, at a soirée, he drew a picture of me on a blackboard, playing his G minor concerto with five hammers, in lieu of fingers, on each hand. The truth of the matter is that I only played his Concerto in G minor from the manuscript, and as I found several of the passages rather simple and not broad enough, if I may use the term, I changed them to suit my own ideas. This, of course, amazed Mendelssohn; who unlike Schumann or Chopin, would never take a hint or advice from anyone. Moreover, Mendelssohn, who, although a refined pianist, was *not* a virtuoso, and could never play my compositions with any kind of effect, his technical skill being inadequate to the execution of intricate passages. So the only course laid open to him, he thought, was to vilify me as a musician.

Liszt also replied to such criticism or censure with his most supreme weapon, the actual quality of his playing. Describing a domestic version of his famous duel with Thalberg he tells us how Mendelssohn played his Fourth Hungarian Rhapsody, "abominably" and then his own F sharp minor Capriccio. Mendelssohn then suggested that Liszt played something "new and striking." The sarcasm was unmistakable and Liszt replied by playing the same Capriccio though "arranged for concert performance." Mendelssohn was totally vanquished "so everything passed over smoothly, and what might have been a very unpleasant meeting turned out a most enjoyable *contretemps*." Needless to say Mendelssohn forgave, but he never forgot.

Reservations of another kind were voiced by Schumann who, though he "trembled and jubilated" at Liszt's titanic virtuosity also noted to his beloved Clara that Liszt's world "is not mine. And as you practise it, and as I often do at the piano when composing, the fine 'inwardness' I would not give up for all his magnificence – and there is somehow, too much tinsel with it all." For Schumann Liszt's Études, for example, suggested extravagance, so much gesturing without genuine poetry or sentiment. Thus, "shall we not envy the boy rather than the man who cannot, it seems, find peace?"

Schumann.

Schumann was too sensitive and intelligent to be merely jealous and yet, like Chopin, he was clearly disturbed by Liszt's pre-eminence. Others naturally interpreted such understandable caution as

envy of his unsurpassable mastery of the keyboard, jealous of the golden harvest of his fingers, scornful at his disregard for strictly scholastic methods, the Kapellmeisters of Leipzig and of Saxony viewed with misgiving the advent of this musical revolutionary.

His technique was to give them many a sleepless night, with fingers playing over the dumb bedclothes in vain emulation of this magician. Those scales, those arpeggios, those thundering octaves – all within reach, but so distant in their effect! Something he had that they could vie with only in dreams; but there it was, to their discomfiture, and they cherished resentment.

Clara Schumann found a lack of diplomacy in Liszt and a no less significant parallel between Liszt's art and his general behaviour,

Clara Schumann.

saying "he does not trouble enough about local conventions and feelings, and so he fares badly in all the papers." She noticed, too, that "although his conversation was intelligent, she soon tired of his restless and insistent vivacity." Clearly, Liszt represented a type alien to both the Schumanns, musicians wary and provoked by his confident assertion, "tradition is laziness."

Liszt's admirers, who lovingly collected his cigar ends and made bracelets out of his broken strings (and there were many) also marvelled in a different way at his high-handedness if opposed. Unable to forget the social slights paid him in his early years, Liszt responded to all further snubs in the grandest of grand manners. He had not forgotten an estimate of him as "particularly vain and pretentious, affecting the fantastic manners of the young Frenchmen of today, and apart from his value as an artist he is quite an insignificant man" – an opinion that lost him a concert to have been given before the Empress of Austria. His reaction over the years was exaggerated but understandable. Diamonds presented by Frederick William IV of Prussia were tossed aside, and since court etiquette forbade personal intercourse between the King of Pianists and the Queen of Spain, Queen Isabella was ignored. Learning of Ludwig I of Bavaria's interest in Lola Montez, Liszt, stung by jealousy, did not invite him to his concerts. Most formidable of all was the now classic rebuke given to Tsar Nicolas of Russia. Aware of the Tsar's contemptuous references not only to his political views but also to the length of his hair Liszt avenged himself in breathtaking style. The Tsar, as was the custom in those days, continued his conversation while Liszt played and, startled by the pianist's sudden and reproving silence, was icily told, "music herself should be silent when Tsar Nicolas speaks." Liszt did a great deal to elevate the lowly status of the musician; only he could have done so with such impudence and hauteur.

Chapter 6

Carolyne von Sayn-Wittgenstein

Meanwhile vengeance of another kind emerged in the form of Marie d'Agoult's first novel, *Nelida.* Here, she exposed her tragic affair to full public view and left no doubt concerning the identity of the true villain. Balzac's singer, Conti, was replaced by Guerman, a painter of lofty democratic ideals nonetheless dazzled by "the brilliant externals of patrician life." All the ups and downs and particularly the downs of Liszt's and Marie's life together were charted with meticulous accuracy, for Marie had little need of invention or artistic licence; it was simply a case of substituting one name for another.

All the same, when Liszt visited Paris in 1861 he met Marie once more. "I kissed her on the brow for the first time for many years and said to her, "Look Marie, but let me say it in the language of the country people. God be with you! Wish me no harm . . . She could not answer me . . . but her tears rained down. Emile Olliver (Blandine's husband) told me that when he was travelling with her in Italy he often saw her crying bitterly in the places that recalled our youth to her. I told her how moved I had been by the memory. Struggling with words, she said, 'I shall always be true to Italy – and to Hungary.'"

However, members of the social élite were scandalised by *Nelida* and wholly confirmed in their view that Liszt was no gentleman. Liszt himself took a coolly detached and elegantly disengaged view of this sorry tale of a *parvenu* upstart installed in an elevated social order, rejected by his mistress for his sake. Feigning admiration for Marie's work, he remarked that any resemblance between Guerman and any known living person was nothing but malicious gossip. But his cold silence when he heard of Marie's death spoke volumes. He never forgave her for this particular and very public attack.

It took more than *Nelida* to alter radically the always uncertain direction of Liszt's life. His sudden decision to relinquish once and for all the superficial rewards of his *glanz* period was yet another instance of his divided nature reacting to its own wildest excesses. Success once

Princess Carolyne von Sayn-Wittgenstein with her daughter Marie.

more seemed empty ("am I condemned without remission to this trade of buffoon and amuser of drawing-rooms?" he exclaimed, no doubt forgetting a characteristically arrogant retort to the Princess Metternich in Vienna. Asked whether he did good business he replied, "only bankers do business, Madam.")

At the same time no dramatic gesture in Liszt's life would be complete without a final twist and it is ironic to note how one woman's insistence on moderation and a more elevated life-style was so successfully replaced by another's.

Liszt met the Princess Carolyne Sayn-Wittgenstein in 1847 while touring in Kiev and almost immediately a new chapter in his life commenced. She was twenty-eight and, like Marie, was married to a boorish if wealthy husband. Again, like Marie, she had feverish literary aspirations, but unlike Marie was more exotic than beautiful.

Naturally, she was moved to distraction by Liszt's playing and Liszt was attracted by her immense wealth (thirty thousand serfs

Marie d'Agoult.

worked on her estates in the Ukraine) and her odd, powerful and earnestly devout personality; her "fantastical being." Unlike Liszt, her sense of direction was unswerving and, like Marie, she longed to sacrifice one life-style for another. So honour, riches, marriage and official blessing were to be replaced by a new position; the guardian angel and guiding light of Liszt's inflammatory genius. Thus,

I kiss your hands and kneel before you, prostrating my forehead to your feet, laying, like the Orientals, my finger on my brow, my lips and my heart, to assure you that my whole mind, all the breath of my spirit, all my heart exists only to bless you, to glorify you, to love you until death and beyond – beyond even death, for love is stronger than death.

And again,

I am at your tiny feet, beloved – I kiss them, I roll myself under the soles of them and place them on the nape of my neck . . . You know that all these things are not Oriental hyperbole but *faits accomplis* . . . You know how I adore you – O dear masterpiece of God . . . so beautiful, so good, so perfect, so made to be cherished, adored and loved to death and madness.

As Peter Raabe put it, the Princess "could express the most intimate of her heart's commotions only in the bombast and fustion of the most high-blown speech; year after year, in letter after letter, she literally shrieked her love into his face."

Weimar in 1850.

The Altenburg in Weimar.

Liszt as conductor.

But Liszt could hardly resist such florid and impassioned declarations of love, particularly when they expressed such lavish praise of his genius or flattered his ego so shamelessly. At all events any hesitancy on his part was swept away by Carolyne's decision to join him in Weimar and commence far-reaching designs for a new life. A thin pretence of respectability was abandoned when Liszt left his hotel and joined Carolyne at the Villa Altenberg, a solid mansion on the outskirts of Weimar, for a life and work of supposedly simple piety and humility. They were joined by Carolyne's daughter and a Scottish governess and only a few of the less gaudy relics of Liszt's life were installed, no doubt as salutary reminders of an unfortunate past and a new beginning. Reputedly, three children were born of this liaison but, far more importantly, the next twelve years were occupied by intense creativity in an atmosphere of cloistered religious fervour. The 'Dante' Symphony, the Symphonic Poems, and the finest piano music (including the B minor Sonata, the Scherzo and March, and the *Weinen Klagen* Variations) were all written at the Altenberg, and under Carolyne's vigilant eye and supervision Liszt aimed to infuse his music with an altogether more poetic spirit; to show less, to quote Carolyne, of the spangles and the big drum.

The influence of a finer craftsman such as Chopin now made itself felt and Liszt also put into effect the most wide-ranging ambitions for Weimar, and for a "new Athens." The town's limitations would be turned to advantage, its provincial position making it a novel and ideal centre for the Arts. Liszt clearly envisaged a sort of *Weltanschauung*; an ideal liaison of music, literature and painting. The opera house, complete with orchestra, chorus and ballet was placed at

Liszt's disposal and his mixture of genius and sheer application quickly made Weimar a world famous centre. Performances took place of Berlioz's *Benvenuto Cellini, Symphonie Fantastique, Harold in Italy, The Damnation of Faust* and *L'Enfance du Christ;* (the last two conducted by the composer) and significant works by Schumann, Weber, Schubert, Raff and, most of all, Wagner.

Lohengrin, Tannhaüser, and *The Flying Dutchman* were all given, and testified to the newest and most abiding concern in Liszt's life. Wagner and Liszt met in 1840 and Wagner's suspicion of Liszt's celebrity thawed when he perceived his immense enthusiasm for his work. Indeed, Liszt's writings on the glories of Wagner prompted one musicologist to exclaim "we can safely say that with this book on *Tannhaüser* and *Lohengrin* he blazed a trail for Wagner . . . " The world

Wagner.

Wagner.

listened; it was as though the curtain had gone up for the first time on the real beauty of each of these works.

Within a remarkably short while Wagner had monopolised a huge amount of Liszt's time, energy and money for the furtherance of his grandiose plans and, no less quickly, he invited Carolyne's suspicions. Wagner may have seemed to Liszt "like Vesuvius in eruption blazing up sheaves of bouquets, pink and lilac" but as has often been noted his friendship with Wagner was one-sided; strength was met with weakness rather than strength; "begun in opportunism their friendship flourished awhile then faded."

But while it is perhaps an exaggeration to claim that Liszt was a Saint directly responsible for the miracle of Wagner's music, it would be true to say that Wagner was prominent among the sycophants who surrounded Liszt at this time in his life. Like Joachim, Wagner was loyal to Liszt when loyalty paid and disloyal when disloyalty paid better. Aided by Liszt he abandoned poverty with aplomb and even his proud mentor was startled by the change brought about by his own generosity. "I am rather worried about the expenses that I am running him into, for there are always a dozen people at dinner at one o'clock and for supper at nine . . . his manner is decidedly masterful and his reserve is ill-disguised. Towards me the exception is complete and absolute."

Carolyne in particular saw such statements as evidence of Liszt's infatuation and gullibility, saw how easily he was flattered and noted in Wagner an essentially provincial taste for luxury and expensive habits. As one observer put it, "cross-gartered Malvolio in his yellow stockings was fantastic enough, but he would have had to yield the palm to Wagner, pyjamade like a chorus-girl in a revue."

Wagner considered Carolyne a "*monstrum in excessum* of brain and heart" adding, "one can't be cross with her for long, only it needs Liszt's matchless temperament to stand such vivacity; with a poor devil like myself it often disagreed. I can't endure the everlasting racket."

Carolyne, on the other hand, was naturally apprehensive about a man whose professions of devotion were hardly disinterested. When Wagner said, "Liszt is more to me than I to him" he may well have meant that Liszt could further his musical ideas by performances of his work. Wagner, on the contrary, could do little for Liszt whose own music was in dire need of serious recognition. At all events Wagner's professions of loyalty were tainted and his letters (like Liszt's) were too effusive to be sincere. He was generous to Liszt in theory only and there is reason to suppose that he suppressed his music in practice.

Understandably, Carolyne disliked what she saw as Liszt's cringing assumption of inferiority to Wagner and remained unimpressed by his clairvoyant insight into Wagner's music. Both she and Wagner viewed each other as unwelcome influences. Wagner, in particular, was amazed by Carolyne's preference and indeed, insistence on a spectacular rather than magical *pianissimo* finish to the 'Dante' Symphony, and it may well be that other, overly demonstrative touches were supplied by her in otherwise satisfactory compositions (for example the bravura alternative conclusion to the Second Ballade).

While Carolyne's interference in Liszt's work provoked suspicion among visiting musicians so did her high-handed assumption of authority in the town where she was once described as "a virago dressed in all the colours of the rainbow." Her social position was, in any case, compromised by her open liaison with a man to whom she was not married and by the Tsar's confiscation of her Russian estates at Woronince, and his refusal to grant her a divorce. They found her

Woronince.

eccentric (the strength of her cigars was infamous) and dictatorial, and her autocratic bearing must have played its part in Liszt's subsequent downfall in Weimar.

The Tsar's decree and authority, both spiritual and temporal, was underlined by the Vatican who took a dim view of such a lax relationship by a supposedly devout adherent of the Catholic faith.

Baudelaire.

Carolyne arrogantly assumed that her work and status would suffice and absolve her from all normal social responsibility. Ordered to return to Russia, she refused and as a consequence her property was sequestrated and she became an exile. Stripped of her prestige, the Princess cut a much less impressive figure in the local community and her liaison with Liszt was viewed with a blanket censure and condemnation. But her automatic *entrée* to social occasions ceased and Liszt's move to the Altenberg went coldly unacknowledged. All invitations continued to be sent to the hotel where he had previously resided and later both he and Carolyne were pointedly ignored at a public function.

Liszt himself gently railed at Carolyne's plans for him saying, "I have no ambition to soar like an eagle or a bird of Paradise. I keep quiet here on earth and put my trust in the life to come. I must therefore protest humbly and sadly against your misjudgement of me."

At the same time, without her perseverance the 'Faust' Symphony might never have been composed, nor the final version of the Transcendental Études completed. The *Harmonies poétiques et religieuses*, too, date from Liszt's meeting with Carolyne and although this set of ten pieces is uneven it includes some of Liszt's greatest music. In the *Bénédiction de Dieu dans la Solitude* ecstasy is not only expressed in a ceaseless elaboration of the principle idea (rather than in traditional classical development) but also both technically and poetically the music already reaches out towards the world of Messiaen's *Vingt Regards sur l'Enfant Jésus. Pensée des morts*, too, (a reworking of the *Harmonies poétiques et religieuses*, originally a single work written in 1834) for all its eccentricity glows with poetic genius and the sombre and magnificent *Funérailles* recalls the hoofbeats of Chopin's Polish cavalry in the central section of his A flat Polanaise and remembers the thirteen martyrs who died in the 1848-9 Hungarian War of Independence.

Certainly Carolyne understood Liszt's weakness and not just the vexed question of his increasing addiction to alcohol.

For twelve years (in Weimar) I had to look after him in this way; I had to do my own work in the same room with him, otherwise he would never have composed any of the works of this period. It is not genius he lacks, but the capacity to sit still – industry, prolonged application. Unless someone helps him in this respect he is impotent; and when the consciousness of his impotence takes possession of him he has to resort to stimulants. This makes his condition still worse and so the vicious circle widens.

Liszt himself paid a heavy price for such enforced isolation and servitude, and from time to time collapsed into fits of depression and lethargy.

I am mortally sad; I can say nothing and listen to nothing. Only prayer can console me and that only now and then; for I can no longer pray with any continuity, however imperiously I may feel the need to do so. May God give me grace to overcome this moral crisis; may the light of His pity lighten my darkness . . . I have made it a habit to pour out the abundance of my heart only in music, which is a sort of mother tongue to me.

Liszt's "moral crisis" was clearly provoked by deprivation and if we have benefited immeasurably from Carolyne's severity, Liszt suffered deeply during the creation of his finest work.

Yet the list of visitors to the Altenberg was long and impressive. Brahms came and wrote to Clara Schumann in 1854 dismissing the

Liszt, 1856.

B minor Sonata as incomprehensible. Anton Rubinstein (who Liszt called Van II, an affectionate allusion to Beethoven), Von Bülow, Joachim, Tausig, Remenyi, Raff; all came to the Altenberg.

However, the most decisive event occurred when Liszt's patron, the Grand Duke Charles Frederick, died in 1853 and was succeeded by the Grand Duke Alexander whose interest lay primarily in the theatre. Liszt's ambitious schemes for Weimar were suddenly threatened by a lack of financial support, and increasing hostility both to his manner and lavish expenditure was openly expressed at a production of Cornelius's opera, *The Barber of Bagdad.* The hisses and jeers of the audience were more than Liszt could bear and in a mood of great bitterness he resigned his position.

New Athens had obstinately remained old Weimar and it had taken Liszt a distressingly short time to realise that the local aristocracy only welcomed his plans provided they did not have to pay for them. His own position became increasingly painful and embarrassing. Repeatedly snubbed by the gentry he remarked in a superbly savage turn of phrase, "courts welcome great men provided they cease to be great the moment they come to court." He also learnt that the raising of musical standards implied criticism.

At the same time it would be difficult to over-estimate Liszt's colossal energy or his sheer achievement in Weimar. He revived a huge repertoire of forgotten works and organised concerts of every kind. The world première of *Lohengrin* took place despite the most pitifully limited revenue, and Liszt's manifesto makes amply clear that his artistic conscience could not allow him to ignore the most progressive elements in music."

either our theatre must express its regret for having performed great tragic and lyrical masterpieces such as *Tannhäuser* and *Lohengrin*, dedicating itself heart and soul to the infernal deities of stagnation, decrepitude and most idiotic banality – or it must go forward, develop and organise all the possible lustre imparted to it in this sense by the director for the last eighteen months.

These were brave and fighting words that fell on deaf ears. For once Liszt's courage failed and he was forced to turn his back on an impossible venture.

It was during this hyperactive if frustrating period that Liszt turned once more to the doctrines of Saint-Simon, rejoicing again in the possibility of a unity of the arts. "I have always dreamt of a renewal in music through a more intimate alliance with poetry, a freer development which would be closer to the spirit of the age. Whatever happens it will triumph unmistakably because it is an integral part of the whole body of just and true ideas of our time."

Liszt saw music as a true moral and liberating force irresistibly communicating ideas as well as emotions, and his *Faust* and *Dante*

Symphonies were the culminating point of his work during this period. The problem of the Faustian man resembled the problem of the Romantic man, and he had given much thought to the question of a dual and ambiguous personality. From the plethora of material in Goethe's epic poem he concentrated on the three principle characters which form the three parts of the Symphony; *Faust, Gretchen* and *Mephistopheles.*

Dante's *Divina Commedia* was also a lifelong influence. Liszt read it at Como with Marie d'Agoult and again with Carolyne at Woronice. The result was once more a tripartite work; Hell, Purgatory and Paradise (later changed on Wagner's advice to an imposing Magnificat). The B minor Sonata is no less a work of Faustian ambition and magnitude and the Gran Mass, his first great piece of church rather than secular music, dates from this time ("I prayed it more than composed it" he wrote to Wagner).

But the critical response to all this music was swift and unforgiving. Liszt's music was found to be more outrageous than novel; musical nonsense posing as music of the future.

Saint-Simon

Liszt.

Mussorgsky.

His music festivals also provoked a mixture of amusement and irritation. Distinguished performances in Ballenstadt, Karlsruhe and the Mozart celebrations in Vienna all involved him in a fight for musical causes and particularly for the music of the Russian 'Five:' the 'Mighty Band' or *phalange intrépide*. Borodin, who visited Weimar in 1877, was deeply moved by Liszt's integrity and commitment to others, thus,

if he accepts someone as his pupil he rarely restricts himself to the formal relations of teacher and pupil; he follows the private lives of his pupils with the warmest interest . . . he shares their joy and troubles, he is affected by their family relationships or love affairs. And how much tenderness, tact, gentleness and kindness pervade his whole being in the art of teaching! I was able to see it with my own eyes and it is my living experience of it which makes me think so highly of Liszt as a man.

The feeling was mutual and Liszt went to some pains to see that the work of Balakirev, Cui, Rimsky-Korsakov, Moussorgsky and particularly Borodin was acknowledged as "worth the serious attention of musical Europe." He may have described Balakirev's Oriental Fantasia, *Islamey* as "a charming Oriental rattle" but he was entirely sympathetic with the Five's avowed aim, "the emancipation of art from subservience to foreign interest and the institution of a national school of music."

More specifically it is interesting to note Borodin's response in his letters to Liszt who was at this time very much the reigning musical monarch. He writes enthusiastically to his wife, describing a local concert in Weimar where Liszt improvised his piano part in a lugubrious arrangement of Chopin's Funeral March for piano, organ and cello. Borodin was overwhelmed by Weimar, with its romantic past and exciting present. Memories of Goethe and Schiller still haunted its streets, and like others before him the nobility of Liszt's presence left an unforgettable impression. After he had sent in his visiting card, "there arose before me as though out of the ground, a tall figure with a long nose, a long black frock coat and long white hair." Frightened of Liszt's response to his originality Borodin was more than reassured by Liszt's words. At his suggestion that he could alter parts of his First Symphony Liszt exclaimed

Heaven forbid! Do not touch it, alter nothing. Your modulations are neither extravagant nor faulty. You have gone far, indeed, and this is precisely your special merit; but you have never made any mistakes. Do not listen to those who would hold you back; believe me, I entreat you, you are on the right road. Your artistic intellect is such that you need not fear to be original. Remember that the same advice was given to Beethoven and Mozart in their day. If they had followed it, they would never have become masters.

Liszt, 1870.

Ferdinand Hiller.

Understandably, such golden words swept all doubts or misgivings aside and Borodin felt "enveloped" by the older man's wisdom, ("I was under his spell and could not sleep") adding, "just fancy, in Weimar many people bow to me who do not know me, because they have seen me with Liszt, and the same at Jena." For Borodin, Weimar was no less than the Venusberg.

Meanwhile Liszt's conducting fell under a no less hostile scrutiny from his enemies than his compositions and piano playing. To Ferdinand Hiller, his one time friend and colleague, Liszt replied, "Hiller's conducting is like his whole personality; accommodating, rounded, correct, even distinguished, but without tension and energy, and consequently without authority or communicative electricity... he might as well be reproached for having no faults, thus giving criticism no foothold." Quick to counter accusations of extravagance or egocentric virtuosity Liszt added, "I think I have clearly explained that to my mind a conductor's real task is to make himself ostensibly almost superfluous. We are pilots, not workers."

Daniel Liszt.

Liszt, *forte et piano*.

Liszt.

Despite such protean activity the strain of the Weimar period was too much, and in a mood of great bitterness Liszt resigned his position. He saw his immense efforts, not only on his own behalf, despised and rejected and this, combined with the sudden death of his son Daniel at the age of twenty, led to some of his darkest hours. A squalid argument with Wagner over the latter's endless demands for money provided a cruel addition to Liszt's sufferings and after his resignation he turned once more to religion for solace. His variations on Bach's Cantata, *Weinen Klagen Sorgen Zagen* bear eloquent witness to his despair, though it is no less characteristic that he could resolve such dramatic despair in a radiantly affirmative conclusion; a desperate credo of his threatened inner faith and life.

Chapter 7

Crisis and Solace

Liszt now entered what was surely the deepest of his many crises. Filled with remorse and contrition he wrote his last will and testament, feeling once more the ultimate call of God, too often neglected in the whirl of his confused and agitated life. Aware again of the divine light of the Cross he paid tribute to Carolyne, regretted his single state which malignant circumstances had forced on him and recalled her dedication to his life and art. Feeling he owed her "the little that I am and the very little that I have" he went on to celebrate Wagner's genius, paused to remember Caroline de Saint Crique (his first love rather than his second for Marie d'Agoult) and finally begged to be "buried simply, without any pomp and, if possible, at night".

In this frame of mind it is hardly surprising that Liszt wished more than ever to legalise and sanctify his relationship with Carolyne, and their marriage was planned to take place in Rome in 1861, on his fiftieth birthday. Alas, it was not to be, for Carolyne's family quickly found reasons for opposition (her husband's fortune on his marriage was now at stake) and so tragically, both were left to go their separate ways, he to the *Villa d'Este*, she to her sunless apartment in Rome. The Catholic Church, despite Carolyne's association with the most elevated officials, also felt unable to sanction their union and so even when Prince Nicolas died, talk of marriage was not resumed. The cynical naturally concluded that Liszt had had second thoughts and, tired of his commitment, again felt the imperious call of freedom. At the same time this unexpected intervention, coinciding with the death of Liszt's daughter Blandine in 1862, must have seemed like a further blight or curse on his existence and so he retired from the world finding a temporary peace as guest of the Vatican. Resident opposite the Loggia of Raphael he cut a strange and, for many, ironic figure prompting the priest Ferdinand Gregorovius to comment, "yesterday I saw Liszt clad as an Abbé. He was getting out of a hackney carriage his black silk cassock fluttering ironically behind him. Mephistopheles disguised as an Abbé." Later he wondered if Liszt was burnt out, that only the wall was still standing in which there flickered a ghostly flame. An oddly incongruous figure, it was jokingly remarked that he belonged to the sights of the Vatican as much as Michelangelo's last judgement or the Belvedere Apollo.

Soon he moved to the cloister of Santa Francesca Romana, looking out onto the Forum and the Temple of Venus, but more importantly he was also a guest of the Dominican friars of the tiny monastery of Madonna del Rosario on the Monte Mario. Perched high above Rome's cupolas and spires this exquisite shrine has been called "a place where one can sense the nearness of eternity", and Liszt's stay there was made doubly fulfilling by the visits of Pope Pius IX to his simple and austere cell. Having felt that his life was wasted and that he had succeeded only "in stammering a few scattered notes which the wind carried away" Liszt was deeply thankful and reassured by the Pontiff's response to the playing of what he called his "dear Palestrina".

The Monastery,
Madonna del Rosario.

The Princess Carolyne
von Sayn-Wittgenstein.

The law, my dear Palestrina, ought to employ your music if, however, she could get it other than in this spot, in order to lead hardened criminals to repentance. Not one could resist it, I am sure; and the day is not far distant, in these times of humanitarian ideas, when similar psychological methods will be used to soften the hearts of the vicious.

The Two Saint Francis Legends date from this period and if Liszt apologised for his lack of ingenuity and asked forgiveness for "impoverishing the wonderful profusion of the text of the 'Sermon to the Birds' both pieces remain astonishingly graphic and original. Saint Francis of Assisi's Sermon to the Birds and Saint Francis of Paola's walk on the waters are essays in musical imagery which could so easily have respectively resulted in mere sentimentality and bombast.

Liszt's vivid if invariably temporary convictions now led him, in 1865, to join the order of Saint Francis, to receive minor orders in the Church and acquire the title of Abbé. Both his admirers and critics were stunned by this step though Liszt remained calm saying, "I think I need hardly tell you that I have not changed to any extent, still less have I forgotten anything. It is only that my life is ordered more simply – and that the Catholic direction of my childhood has become a regular and guiding sentiment."

Liszt received four out of the seven degrees of the priesthood allowing his general life-style (austere enough at the time) to remain unaltered and uncircumscribed. Ironically, he was even allowed to marry.

Yet once more the cynics could hardly ignore this extreme change of direction and suspected more of a publicity stunt than the action of a sincere or devout man. Even the endearing *Pio Nono*, after listening for five hours to Liszt's confession on becoming an Abbé, brusquely exclaimed, "*Basta, caro* Liszt! go and tell the rest of your sins to the piano."

However, Liszt's extra-musical and religious activities were rare indeed, and only the death of his mother in 1866 took him away to her funeral in Paris, where he also heard a performance of his Mass for Gran Cathedral. He also journeyed to Budapest the following year for a performance of his Hungarian Coronation Mass, where he received an overwhelming reception and founded the Franz Liszt Academy of Music. At this time in his life his every move was lovingly charted and never more so than in his native country. His religious retreat, so far from discouraging interest or curiosity, had fanned it to an ever greater intensity and his appearance in Budapest could hardly have been more dramatic. Describing the crowds waiting to see Francis Joseph on his way to his coronation as apostolic King of Hungary, Janka Wohl describes an even more remarkable appearance.

St Francis of Paola
walking on the waves.

When the feverish suspense grew intense, the tall figure of a priest, in a long
black cassock studded with decorations, was seen to descend the broad white
road leading to the Danube, which had been kept clear for the royal
procession. As he walked bareheaded, his snow-white hair floated on the
breeze, and his features seemed cast in brass. At his appearance, a murmur
arose which welled and deepened as he advanced and was recognised by the
people. The name of Liszt flew down the serried ranks from mouth to mouth,
swift as a flash of lightning. Soon a hundred thousand men and women were
frantically applauding him with the excitement of this whirlwind of voices.
The crowd on the other side of the river naturally thought it must be the
King, who was being hailed in the spontaneous acclamation of a reconciled
people. It was not *the* King but it was *a* King, to whom were addressed the
sympathies of a grateful nation proud of the possession of such a son.

Title page for the Two Legends.

Liszt always retained a brilliant and theatrical sense of occasion and it is perhaps hardly surprising that after a further retreat, accompanied by the Abbé Solfanelli, this time to Grotta Mare on the Adriatic, Liszt's serenity gave way to other increasingly urgent demands. The world beckoned once more and, provoked out of retirement by the entirely worldly matter of his daughter's elopement with Wagner, he again commenced a life of restless travel, activity and endeavour.

Chapter 8

La Vie Trifurqée

Liszt's *Vie trifurqée*, his peripatetic existence between Rome, Weimar and Budapest, became a symbol of a triple quest; the intellectual groping for spiritual faith, the artist seeking a cosmopolitan and universal vehicle of expression, and the lifelong emigré looking for his national roots. Dividing his time between these cities Liszt's relationships with all three places radically altered. He arrived in Weimar, for example, unaccompanied by Carolyne (always a cause of acrimony) and with no official directorship of the town's music. The *Altenberg* was replaced by the *Hofgärtnerei*, a spacious and comfortable villa that amply fulfilled his needs as a greatly celebrated teacher. Liszt's position was essentially that of an honoured guest.

Carolyne was kept more or less informed of Liszt's life but an episode in 1869, dramatic even by Liszt's standards, must have confirmed her worst fears. Olga Janina, a nineteen year old Russian 'Countess' came to Rome and, attracted by her exceptional vivacity rather than by her slender musical talent, Liszt accepted her as a student.

Neither Cossack nor Countess, Olga Janina, whose real name was Zielimska, married at fifteen and horsewhipped her husband before leaving him on the second day of their marriage. She became a mother at sixteen and was later deported by the police from Budapest. A pathological case, she nonetheless followed in the line of many other women when she found Liszt's smile to be "like a shaft of sunlight". Predictably, her attendance at his master-classes was soon supplemented with private lessons. However, an uncharacteristic element of caution on Liszt's part made him hesitate before committing himself to her and yet another precarious relationship. Made apprehensive by Olga's clearly desperate nature or simply bitten so many times that he was more than twice shy, he retreated before her advances to the *Villa d'Este* in Tivoli outside Rome where amid the scintillating brilliance of fountains and spray he hoped for

Liszt's house at the entrace to the park in Weimar.

uninterrupted periods of peaceful and grave meditation.

But such ideal seclusion was shattered by Olga's arrival. Disguised as a gardener's boy she coaxed admission, and Liszt, jaded by his prolonged isolation, welcomed her with open arms. Suitably equipped, Olga's plan was to kill Liszt should he rebuff her affections once more. Fortunately his declaration of love put a temporary stop to this campaign and so Liszt, like a man with a ball and chain, continued his journeys with Olga attached. Once more his activities provoked ribald comments as well as censure from a visiting Cardinal who was deeply offended by Olga's exceptional freedom and familiarity.

The affair continued until this latest and oddest of Liszt's ladies performed at one of his student recitals and provoked his public wrath by her incompetence. Liszt berated her without mercy and after taking a heavy dose of laudanum she slept for forty-eight hours and was assumed dead. She then revived with her considerable energy recharged and after a further and even colder dismissal by her erstwhile lover decided to kill both herself and Liszt. Once more her plan failed and she returned to Paris to write her memoirs where she attempted a predictably *grand exposé*. Her *Memoirs d'une Piano, Les Amours d'une cosaque pour un ami de l'Abbé or Le Roman du pianiste et la cosaque*, written under such pseudonyms as Robert Franz or Sylvia Zorelli once more depicted Liszt in the thinnest of disguises, and Olga made certain that copies were sent to all her friends including the Pope.

Liszt's account of this appalling episode (amusing only in retrospect) was naturally circumspect and Carolyne was left to pause briefly in her gargantuan literary task (her twenty-five volume opus *Les Causes intérieures de la faiblesse extérieure de L'Église*) to shake her head sadly at her lover's inconstancy and reckless disregard for safety.

Olga Janina (alias Madame Césano née Princesse Orbeliani).

Liszt was, however, cautious regarding *Les Causes*, the *stupendo libro*, as he called it. He read the one thousand two hundred and seventy seven pages of the first two volumes, and their excitable and contentious style made him fear criticism and possibly excommunication from the Church. His worst suspicions were confirmed in 1877 when the Sacred Congregation of the *Index Expurgatoris* issued a decree prohibiting circulation of the *Causes* among the clergy. The fifth volume in particular caused considerable annoyance, yet Carolyne continued with the other nineteen,

The cover of *Memories of a Pianist*.

Olga Janina as Madame Césano.

Liszt and his pupils, including such celebrated pianists as Siloti, Arthur Friedheim, Emil von Sauer and Moriz Rosenthal.

completing the twenty-fourth a few days before her death in 1887.

Meanwhile, in Weimar Liszt gained a unique and world-wide reputation for his teaching. And if Liszt was the first authentic concert pianist and the first to perform from memory he was also the first to give what are now popularly known as "master-classes"; an institution admirably geared to blend instruction with flattery of his always susceptible ego. Liszt charged no fee and asked only that his students should come soundly equipped in all technical matters, leaving him free to discuss only the higher readers of interpretation and style. Such a setting would have been surprising if it had not included a touch of grandeur. Liszt's students quickly became his disciples and devotees, and at four o'clock precisely his entrance was greeted with a hushed awe and reverence. Amy Fay, most articulate and delightful of his followers, noted the way a Mephistophelian touch mingled with "a sort of Jesuitical elegance and ease".

Liszt, 1867.

Anything so perfectly beautiful as he looks when he sits at the piano I never saw, and yet he is almost an old man now. His personal magnetism is immense, and I can scarcely bear it when he plays. He can make me cry all he chooses . . . he knows well the influence he has on people, for he always fixes his eye on some one of us when he plays, and I believe he tries to wring our hearts.

94

Borodin was no less enchanted, noting that "evidently he has a weakness for the fair sex" as Liszt went through his elaborate preliminary courtesies with one of his students. "Liszt tapped Mademoiselle Imanov kindly on the cheek and kissed her on the forehead while she kissed his hand; this is the custom between Liszt and his pupils."

At the same time Borodin must have been no less intrigued by Liszt's effortless assumption of superiority. When a student of Tausig, and Nicolas Rubinstein suggested playing Chopin's Third Sonata and the Schumann Fantasie, Liszt exclaimed

Oh certainly *not* the Sonata. I never allow students to play that incomparable *chef d'oeuvre*; you see, my dear young friend, it is one of those musical creations which should *only* be played at certain times and under certain conditions. Personally I prefer to play it when absolutely alone. The inspirations of this marvellously beautiful Sonata spring from a fount of deepest melancholy and are best suited to solitary reflection. As to *hearing* it played there is but one pianist living whom I consider worthy of interpreting it; and that is Anton Rubinstein.

A performance of the Schumann Fantasie, too, became unthinkable after Liszt had told this "young and rising artist" that he himself had played it to Schumann and had been praised to the skies. And as if to underline this formidable point he then played *Traumes Wirren* from the *Fantasiestücke*, opus 12, with a staggering ease and rapidity. After such remarks and displays it would have been foolhardy indeed to have played anything!

Another luckless young American student who had the temerity to ask Liszt if he knew any of Mendelssohn's music was told, "a little", before being offered the following advice.

And do not forget another thing; when you have attained to the heights of virtuosity and intellectual possibilities, you have not finished your work. For to remain at this dizzying altitude of artistic possibility you have to continue your daily slavery, otherwise your highly trained muscles and nerves and brain will relax to a more normal tension. It is this fact which so often disgusts the executive artist. I have locked my piano and given up music altogether. But the love of Art returns of its own accord and with an unmistakeable yearning, such as only those to the manner born can feel and enjoy.

Liszt fluently assumed the role of *grand seigneur* and, like royalty, he alone was allowed to open a conversation. Nonetheless virtually all who flocked to attend his lessons recalled their incomparable nature. And although Liszt was inclined to recommend the local sights and the excellence of other teachers to his less gifted students his kindness and concern were no less rightly celebrated. He was full of comforting words for those who attracted a poor audience for their first and important recitals, reminding them that he had had similar disappointments. He was quick to tell them, too, that the large audience that attended his second concert had come for extra musical reasons, and discovering that he had five fingers on each hand rather than the rumoured six, left in a state of indifference. Liszt, they felt, was after all just an ordinary pianist.

But to have heard Liszt play in such an informal setting must have been unforgettable. And it was in Rome that one student recalled the old wizard casting his unqiue spell once more,

he played the Schubert Serenade. It was simple, quiet and clear, like a beautiful moonlight evening. Then he let himself go for the last time, and we heard the cadenza, like awakening nightingales who burst into songs of longing and joy, of love and exaltation . . .

Another admirer said,

as he grew older, his playing seemed infinitely more significant than when I heard him at the time of his great concert successes. Such calm, such spiritual depth irradiated and transfigured his playing as seemed to liberate him from the limitations of the instrument and fill it with a magic I never found in any other pianist I heard.

Reminiscence concerning his friendship with, say, Chopin or Schumann, too, must have been extraordinary and a vital contact from the past, for unlike those two very different apostles of Romanticism Liszt lived on to know another age. In works such as *Jadis* (which roughly translated means, 'formerly') the *Four Valses oubliée*, or the *Romance oubliée*, Liszt created music of an elusive, bitter-sweet potency, reflections not so much in tranquillity but in dark moods made all the more disturbing by the novel economy with which they were expressed. Such pinpoint delicacy and ambiguous emotion, subtly distanced, are a far cry from the prophetic dawn of a new anti-romanticism in, say, the percussiveness, angularity and entirely 'unvocal' treatment of the piano of the *Totentanz*, the last three Mephisto Waltzes or the *Toccata* (already a close relation of Shostakovitch's Prelude from the A minor Prelude and Fugue).

It was, incidentally, Borodin who described the *Totentanz* as "the most powerful of all works for piano and orchestra for its originality of idea and form, for the beauty, depth and power of its theme, the novelty of its interpretation, its profoundly religious and mystical sentiment, its Gothic and liturgical character". After listening to such fulsome praise Liszt wryly remarked that the *Totentanz* was considered a fiasco in Germany.

Grieg was also among the visitors to Weimar and his Piano Concerto betrays the strongest Lisztian bias (notably in the cadenza). In 1870 Grieg wrote to his parents quoting Liszt's words which were

Liszt, 1886.

strongly reminiscent of Liszt's advice to Borodin, ". . . continue on your way; I tell you, you have the gift. Don't let yourself be deterred". Grieg never forgot this encouragement, saying,

this last remark had an inexpressible significance for me. There was something in it that might be called consecration. Whenever I am disappointed and bitter I shall remember those words and the memory of that hour will preserve its wonderful power and support me in the days of misfortune.

Albéniz also came to Weimar and his four books of *Iberia* bristle with difficulties which, for all their lavish poetic novelty, surely derive from an essentially Lisztian sense of pianistic complexity.

These, together with virtually every pianist of note before the public between 1870 and 1910, all came to Weimar. Rosenthal, Tausig, Bülow, Siloti and Friedheim, among others, formed the peerage of the realm of pianists.

Liszt's stay in Budapest was no less remarkable and the opening of the Liszt Academy in 1875 provided some consolation for the collapse

The Triumph of Death.

of his hopes in Weimar in 1858. As far back as 1838, rallying to his country's cause, Liszt had expressed his feeling with the most fervent show of patriotism.

Nature in her grandeur spread herself out before my eyes; I saw the Danube dashing over the rocks; I saw vast grassy plains on which thousands of sheep were peacefully browsing! It was Hungary, that generous and fertile land which had reared a noble race! And I also, I exclaimed, in a burst of patriotism at which perhaps you will smile, and I also am a member of this brave and indomitable nation which will yet see more happy days!

Small wonder that Liszt became a symbol and rallying cry in Hungary's ferment of poetry and politics, a symbol recalled in an

"Ode to Franz Liszt".

"Famous musician of the world
True to this country wherever you go,
Have a voice amidst the mighty swell
and fervour of your piano strings
For your sick country too?"

Understandably, Liszt's symphonic poem *Hungaria* and his transcription of the Rákóczy March caused a patriotic furore that suitably underlined his proud declaration,

despite my lamentable ignorance of the language, I must be permitted to remain from birth to death, in heart and soul a Hungarian, and hence I am anxious to promote the cause of Hungarian music.

Liszt's Nineteen Hungarian Rhapsodies, a national epic to the Magyar disposition, form his most generous, sparkling and flamboyant tribute. Their gypsy origins also derive from Liszt's attraction for the unconventional and anti-establishment. For so romantic a figure their distinctive qualities proved irresistible,

their primitivism, supposed prophetic talent and erotic and barbarous charm; the folk quality of their culture and finally their nomadic and unbourgeoise way of life which affronted both the middle class respect for the law and its prized sense of property.

In a sense the glamour of the exotic or remote appealed to Liszt's nature, and distance certainly lent Hungary an enchantment, colour and robustness she may not have acquired had he spent the better part of his life there. As it was, he always wished to be considered Hungarian, though, characteristically, he was both ardent nationalist and sophisticated cosmopolitan combined.

At the same time it would be impossible to underestimate the Hungarian or Magyar influence and as early as 1822 Liszt was mesmerised by the gypsy violinist, Janos Bihari.

I was just beginning to grow up when I heard this great man . . . He used to play for hours on end, without giving the slightest thought to the passing of time . . . His musical cascades fell in rainbow profusion, or glided along in a soft murmur . . . His performances must have distilled into my soul the essence of some generous and exhilarating wine; for when I think of his playing, the emotions I then experienced were like one of those mysterious elixirs concocted in the secret laboratories of those alchemists of the Middle Ages.

In a sense the Hungarian Rhapsodies are an evocation of a childhood memory, tinged (in the case of Nos. 16-19) with bitterness and regret.

Chapter 9

The Final Years

Liszt's fame and celebrity continued unabated and with increasing recognition. But the clear skies that had opened up to him were shadowed by a no less immediate awareness of isolation and imminent death. Most of his closest friends and colleagues had died – Ingres in 1867, Berlioz in 1869 and the never-to-be-forgotten Caroline de Saint Cricq in 1872, (the deaths of George Sand and Marie d'Agoult disturbed him far less).

On Marie's death in 1876 he wrote,

short of hypocrisy I wouldn't weep more over her death than over her life. La Rochfoucauld has truly said that hypocrisy is homage paid to a victim; but it is preferable to prefer true homage to false. Now Madame d'Agoult had pre-eminently the taste and even the passion for the false, except in certain moments of exaltation of which she could not bear to be reminded.

Fêted and admired, Liszt was also strongly conscious of relentless opposition from so many quarters – even in far away Cincinnati where he was asked to conduct in 1870. Answering an invitation to conduct the Music Festival in that city he replied,

I must unfortunately ask you to give my sincere apologies to the Honourable Committee. I am so much too old to undertake such a task satisfactorily . . .

I thank you for the invitation and especially for the performances of my works in America where they are very often much criticised and sometimes abhorred! Also many thanks to Mr Thomas for his performances of my works.

This sad and touching letter reminds us that Liszt once listed those countries unresponsive or hostile to his music. Writing in 1854 he said, a hail of press reviews pelts my compositions, not only in Vienna, but even to the same extent in Russia and America. On all sides, in Leipzig and Berlin and along the Rhine, in St. Petersburg and New York, learned critics have declared that it is a crime and an offence against art to approve of my compositions or even to hear them without first condoning them . . . I sometimes have grave doubts about composing further. Yet I will not give up, though I doubt if I can express what is hovering in my innermost self.

Such writing predates another great Hungarian composer's fears. Bartók always felt for the well-being of performers intrepid enough to present his music to the public and, like Liszt, saw himself as a classic whipping-boy, hurt and dismayed however broad his shoulders. Certainly, the composer who had so bravely advised others to fight against adversity was himself the target of sustained hostility and incomprehension. Liszt had become more than a dubious figure in his old age; more a genius debased to the level of a buffoon.

More cheerfully, Liszt's friendship with Wagner was thankfully resumed after an eleven year break, and in 1876 he attended the opening of Bayreuth. Liszt's belief in Wagner's genius was unfaltering, thus,

The Wagner Theatre, Bayreuth.

Cosima Liszt (later
Cosima Wagner).

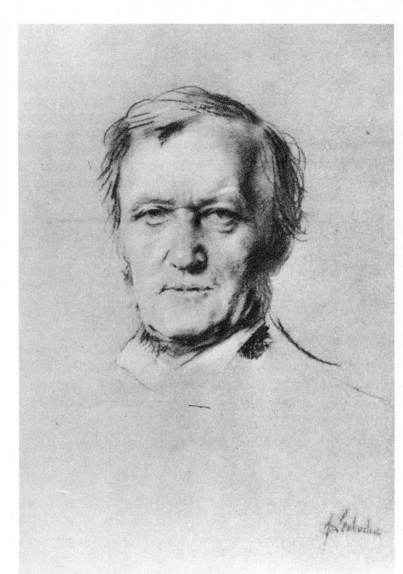

Wagner.

Richard Wagner is the greatest musical genius born in the century, and possibly in any other. He is far the greatest tone painter that has ever existed. Also as a musical delineator of emotion, grief and ecstasy he stands totally alone, apart and ahead of any other composer who has so far lived. His knowledge of the orchestra, and his power of handling it has never been surpassed, if ever equalled; his melodies entrance the listener with an almost supernatural charm... and are full of the most subtle, emotional and delicate effects, which are an everlasting fount of inspiration alike to performer and listener. In 'Parsifal' he reached the zenith of his powers; there is no composition extant which can compare with it, either in power of wondrous melody, in purity of musical expression, in magnificence of construction, in perfection of orchestration. It is a veritable *chef d'oeuvre*.

Ferruccio Busoni.

Visits to Rome continued and formed a *vie trifurgée* in themselves, divided between Tivoli, Carolyne's all but uninhabitable apartment, and other friends who remained in the city. At Tivoli, with its magical background of cascading fountains and wind-blown cypresses (the tranquil and ironic setting of that near fatal encounter with Olga Janina) he lived and composed music for another age, resigned if hardly indifferent to the outside world's scorn and derision. Here, he wrote the third book of his *Années de Pèlerinage* where the wind is heard sighing through the funeral trees and *les Jeux d'eau à la Villa d'Este*, inspired by mystical and religious symbolism and considered by no less a figure than Busoni to be the father of all musical fountains.

Made doubtful of such music's validity Liszt wrote, "Oh, how dry and unsatisfactory the sorrow and lamentation of almighty Nature sounds on the piano – or even on the orchestra – unless it be Wagner's or Beethoven's!" Yet such doubts must have been temporary for Liszt also completed at this time the hauntingly elusive Fsharp Impromptu, part of the oratorio Saint Stanislaus, the whole of the *Via Crucis* and the Legend of Cecilia. In 1879 Liszt was installed as Canon of Albano, an honour that must have delighted and surprised him and provided a deep and necessary solace in his old age.

At the same time Liszt was nearing seventy and the strain of his incessant activity began to tell. Less in control of each situation than before he was unaware that an assortment of parasites and sycophants had infiltrated his classes, and it took his son-in-law, Hans von Bülow to remove them and restore a sense of order. Such help enabled Liszt to settle once more into a happy routine clouded only by increasingly weary and autumnal thoughts. Carolyne wrote from Rome,

The Vendramin Palace, Venice.

Carolyne von
Sayn-Wittgenstein
in Rome, 1876.

Cosima Wagner.

Dear, dear good soul, may your seventieth anniversary begin under the auspices of the sun that brightened the twenty-second of October at Woronice. Let us thirst for eternity. It is for eternity that I have desired to possess you in God and give you to God. A good year and many good years, dear great man . . .

a simple and heartfelt tribute that somehow forgave and celebrated so much.

Liszt then journeyed to Venice to be with Wagner and Cosima and in the Vendramin Palace was given all the freedom and comfort he could wish. He attended Mass each morning in the neighbouring church and with an increasing sense of isolation worked at music of the strangest prophecy and sombre, attenuated beauty. It has, incidentally, been suggested that Liszt's obsession with death in so

105

much of his 'late' period dates from 1832 when he witnessed a massive and horrific cholera epidemic in Paris. The sheer extent of the scene was graphically described by Heine who, watching coffins overturn and burst open, in the general despair and confusion wrote, "I seemed to see that most horrible of all *émeutes* – a riot of the dead." *Nuages Gris* (later much admired by both Debussy and Stravinsky) *La Lugubre Gondole* 1 and 2 and *Am Grabe Richard Wagner - Venezia* – a curious, funereal and elliptical meditation on his setting and companions of the time – all date from Liszt's final period.

Most of Liszt's late compositions, including the two *Elégies, Unstern* and the *Three Csardas*, are somehow intimately connected with death and possess a curious bitterness and despair, a bleakness expressed in

Liszt, 1882.

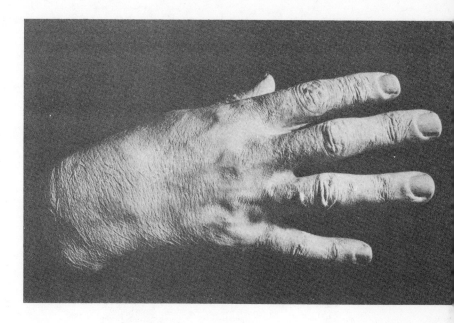

Liszt's hand.

the change from *l'exubérance de coeur* to *l'amertume de coeur*. Compare, for example, the worlds of *La Campanella* and *Angelus*, the one an excuse for the most outgoing brilliance and virtuosity, the other evoking a mysterious and cloistered seclusion of the spirit.

The dark-hued romanticism of this period at once suggests a particular state of mind and soul, a deep despair that not even the Church could ease let alone erase. Wagner's death in 1883 was particularly hard to bear ("He today, I tomorrow") and in a state of the utmost weariness, physical and mental exhaustion he wrote to Carolyne,

It would be better for me not to go out this evening, my fatigue in living is extreme and, in spite of my wish to do so, I no longer feel good for anything. Do not send an answer to this letter.

A final visit to the Princess was inevitable and was followed by a last and surprising resurgence of energy. In 1886 Liszt visited England once more, stopping *en route* in Liège where his Credo for his Gran Mass received an ovation. Still further success followed in Paris, and in London he was greeted with a touching warmth and regard.

There Liszt, bearing his years bravely, and conspicuous by his stature and the extraordinary profusion of snow-white hair falling in masses upon his shoulder, became the centre of attention, the object of an all-absorbing interest. This benevolent-looking amiable smiling patriarch was, then, the extraordinary individual whose personality had exerted for upwards of half a century so vastly dominating an influence over the fortunes of European music.

107

Carolyne von
Sayn-Wittgenstein's
tomb in Rome.

Liszt, 1881.

Liszt returned to Paris in relatively good spirits but, making a final pilgrimage to Bayreuth became seriously ill. Sitting opposite to Liszt on the train and gazing raptly through an open window at the romantic landscape a young couple unwittingly subjected Liszt to intense cold and, whether apocryphal or not, this story has a strange aptness.

Yet with probably the most remarkable instance of fortitude and generosity Liszt insisted on attending a performance of *Tristan*.

With a final and crushing irony, not one of Liszt's works was heard throughout the Festival. Ill and dying, there was no place for him in Wagner's sun. The man who once stood accused by Chopin of allowing him a place only within his Empire, was now himself totally

excluded. Only his most devoted friends attended to his needs but on his death there was no Requiem Mass and he was not buried as he had requested in the habit of the Third Order of Saint Francis.

It was perhaps a crowning irony that Liszt should strenuously journey in his seventy-eighth year to Bayreuth to witness the fulfilment of his dream for another musician – someone he tirelessly supported over a period of forty years – and find himself isolated and ignored; a victim of Wagnerian fanaticism.

Liszt's condition quickly worsened and he was unable to stay to the end of the performance of *Tristan*. Forbidden his brandy (his usual and often successful recourse against illness) he caught pneumonia and became delirious. He died peacefully late at night on July 31, 1886, his heart and mind full of his friend's music, the word 'Tristan' on his lips.

The following year Carolyne completed the twenty-fourth and final volume of her *Causes*, the ultimate *magnum opus* written over a period of twenty-five years, and, her Herculean and unreadable task accomplished, she died two weeks later.

Liszt's tomb in Bayreuth.

Index

Illustrations are indicated in bold type

Other titles in the series